To Mehe
Best wishes
H. Newton Malony
February 1990

Resolving Church Conflicts

A Case Study Approach for Local Congregations

◆

G. DOUGLASS LEWIS

1817

Harper & Row, Publishers, San Francisco

Cambridge, Hagerstown, New York, Philadelphia
London, Mexico City, São Paulo, Sydney

to
Shirley
Laura
and
Doug

FIRST EDITION

Designed by Jim Mennick

Library of Congress Cataloging in Publication Data

Lewis, Granville Douglass, 1934–
   Resolving church conflicts.

   1. Church controversies—Case studies.
I. Title.
BV652.9.L48   1981   254   80-8347
ISBN 0-06-065244-6

---

89 90   10 9 8 7 6 5

Contents

Series Preface
Experience and Reflection
A Case Method Series

The series, Experience and Reflection, seeks to consolidate methodological gains from experimentation with the case method in theological education, both in seminaries and churches. It offers a variety of actual cases together with interpretive materials that aid in the study. Some of the writings are expressly designed for development of one particular aspect of theological education—Bible study, for example. Others are more generally focused to assist persons and communities in their process of religious maturation.

In the last decade the use of inductive educational methods in theological education has increased dramatically; it has become a new mode of instruction in many seminaries and churches. Now, the publication of case-centered works in various areas will provide resources for teaching in seminaries, in congregations, and in other learning situations. The books will also serve those studying religions and ethical traditions in colleges and other settings of continuing education.

ROBERT A. EVANS, PH.D.
Hartford, Connecticut

LOUIS B. WEEKS, PH.D.
Louisville, Kentucky
Series Editors

Preface

I am often asked, "Why do you teach and consult so much with individuals and institutions that are in conflict? How did you get started in this area?" My response is twofold. First, I wanted to learn more about managing conflict in my own life so I began teaching others how to do it. Teaching, I have discovered, is the surest way to learn. The teacher is never the all-knowing expert, immune to the effects of the learning situation. Teacher and students are learners together, colleagues in the quest. In this way, learning and growing are not only more effective, but more fun as well. Second, the subject matter is always relevant to any individual, group, or institution. All of us are born to conflict. It pervades our lives, confronts us at every turn. People are hungry, sometimes even desperate, to learn about managing conflict.

This book does not pretend to have the authorative answer, a bold blueprint for certain success. Its insights, suggestions, and principles have emerged from a lot of experience, much of it my own, and much of it shared with me by others. This experience is combined with theory to provide a framework and a process for understanding and dealing with conflict.

The purpose of the book is to aid individuals and institutions in becoming more effective managers of conflict. It is based on the belief that all of us have or can develop the capacity to experience and use conflict so that it becomes a stimulus to our growth and development toward wholeness rather than a destructive and debilitating influence in our lives and relationships. Our assumptions are fundamental to how we deal with conflict. What we believe about ourselves and our resources, about other persons and their resources, and about conflict as negative or positive will ultimately determine how we act in conflict.

The format of the book is designed to integrate theory and practice—in fact, this is basically a book about theory that constantly moves toward practice. Understanding the theory is a necessary first step, of course, but the payoff lies in how one puts the theory into practice in his or her life. The first part of the book concentrates on theory (but even there its underlying impetus is to move the reader toward practicing it). The second part contains a series of cases, "slices of life" that serve as an intermediate arena between talking about the theory and practicing it in daily life. The cases provide settings that are safer and less risky than real-life situations in which to grapple with conflict issues, test the theory, practice the principles, and discover things about one's own conflict management style. The final step, the ultimate payoff, is not included in this book. It is the application of the theory in practice within one's life. My wish for all users of this material is that it ultimately makes a difference in how they manage conflict in their lives.

The theory of conflict and its management in the book is intended to apply to all settings in human life, but the focus of its illustrations and applications is the church. The church, as an institution and its members, often has more difficulty with conflict because of several of its key assumptions about the nature of love, self-giving, and prohibitions against anger, hate, and hostility. The book addresses these issues directly and challenges the church to deal with conflict differently within itself and to train its members to manage conflict more creatively in the world.

The number of persons who have contributed to the development of the ideas and designs in this book are too numerous to name. Many of their names I never knew, but our lives crossed, sometimes in conflict, often as teachers and learners together, always as unique persons, usually searching after that wholeness for which God created us. To all of them I want to express my appreciation for what they shared of their lives with me and what I learned from them.

Special words of appreciation must go to Rhea Gray, an old friend who launched me many years ago on this inquiry into conflict. My colleagues at Hartford Seminary have provided an extraordinary community for support and growth. Gilda Simpson and Amy Beveridge typed and proofread the manuscript at various stages. Audrey Ermakovich, secretary, friend, and critic, contributed much labor and care to the project. Without the pushing, encouraging, and critiquing of Bob and Alice Evans these ideas would never have gotten translated from talk to print. Louis Weeks was also most helpful and prompt as an editor. Finally, special love and appreciation go to my wife, Shirley, and to my two teenage children, Laura and Doug, whose love, support, and willingness to engage me in conflict have pushed me to become the person I am. They helped to make this book possible in so many ways. This book is dedicated to them.

Part I

A Theory of Conflict and Its Management

<>

Introduction

The unlike is joined together, and from differences results the most beautiful harmony, and all things take place by strife.

HERACLITUS (540–480 B.C.), Fragment 46

The words of Heraclitus, written centuries ago, remind us that differences, strife, and conflict are at the heart of reality. Heraclitus is optimistic about that fact, though; he assumes beautiful harmony can result. Not everyone responds so positively to the conflictual quality of reality, nor is everyone so optimistic that the results are positive. The experience of the tragic and destructive character of existence often weighs against the idea of positive possibilities.

The question for humans existing in this reality is, Can we do anything about it? Do we have any control? Can we shape reality in a positive or negative direction? The answer is yes and no. We are victims, the recipients without choice of much that life offers, but we also have an option about how we respond. This book recognizes and affirms the inevitability of conflict in human existence, but it assumes that we have the capacity to influence and shape, within the realm of human

interaction, whether that conflict will be destructive or constructive. We *can* learn to manage conflict creatively and
constructively.

The approach to learning taken in the book assumes that we
learn cognitively, behaviorally, and emotionally, and that all
three modes must be included in a complete learning process.
Much of current conflict management training is designed to
place people in conflict so that they experience conflict emotionally and then reflect on how they responded behaviorally.
The training focuses on identifying feelings and practicing new
behaviors. Such training tends to ignore the cognitive dimension of learning and changing. It fails to recognize that persons
act according to a set of concepts and assumptions about what,
from their perspective, is appropriate and fulfilling to them.

These chapters take into account all three dimensions of
learning. Part I provides a theory about conflict and its management and points to some of the behavioral and emotional
implications of this theory. Part II provides cases through
which individuals can apply the theory and test it behaviorally
and emotionally.

Chapter 1 sets forth a model for understanding human interaction and the emergence of conflict. It discusses the nature of
conflict, its inevitability in human existence, and the destructive consequences of an avoidance style of dealing with conflict.

Chapter 2 brings the perspective of Christian faith to bear on
understanding and dealing with conflict. Much of contemporary conflict management theory, including that applied to the
church, has arisen out of the behavioral sciences. The rich resources of the Christian faith—its perspective on life and its
tragic elements, and its vision of wholeness—have often been
neglected or misused by the church in dealing with conflict.

Chapter 3 proposes principles for creative conflict management. The principles are intended as guidelines, or reminders,
of essential attitudes, skills, and methods for dealing creatively
and effectively with conflict. The guidelines integrate theory
and practice.

Chapter 4 points out that individuals have certain styles or
fixed patterns of dealing with conflict. To manage it more cre-

atively, one must become aware of how he or she habitually reacts in conflict. In addition to a framework for understanding conflict management styles, the chapter proposes a method for changing styles that are unsatisfactory and ineffective.

CHAPTER 1

The Nature of Conflict

When my daughter Laura was five, she loved to play with cardboard boxes. A big box would occupy her for hours. She would crawl into it, sit inside it, or hide under it. One day when a friend came to play, their activity centered around a modest-sized box. After watching Laura sit in the box, Josh naturally wanted to get in as well. He gave Laura a shove and she reciprocated. A shoving match followed. Soon they were hitting each other, screaming, and crying. The escalation of the conflict and noise level prompted me to intervene and suggest some alternatives. The children listened and cooperated. They took turns—one sat in the box, the other rocked it to give the effect of a carnival ride, and vice versa. Next, one hid somewhere in the room and the one in the box crawled out to search for the hidden one. Finally, with some help from me, both squeezed into the box together. This alternative brought great joy. They finally learned to get into the box together without outside assistance, which pleased them even more.

It occurred to me years later that this encounter between two children offers a paradigm of human conflict that raises fundamental issues and questions about both the nature of conflict and its management. Why did the children get into a conflict over the box? Is conflict inevitable? What is it about humans that invariably gets us into conflict? Need this conflict always be negative? How can it be managed better? These questions, which clearly apply to the conflict over the box, are also applicable to the conflicts with which all of us regularly struggle.

CONFLICT: A DEFINITION

Some persons operate on the "limited resources" theory of conflict. If in their minds only one box exists, and only one party can get in the box, why shouldn't it be they? Their efforts to possess the box may produce hostility in others but, they reason, such is the price of achievement. They are, nevertheless, in touch with the two key elements in conflict. First, there is always a box or space both parties want to occupy. The box represents whatever they are competing for: material goals, opportunities for advancement, recognition, status, territory, or the attention of others. The second element is the intention or goal of each party. If either did not want to occupy the space or the box, there would be no conflict.[1] As with dancing, so with conflict—it takes two to tango. The limited resources view of conflict is, I believe, mistaken in its management assumption—that only one can get into the box—but more on that later.

Incorporating both components, personal intentions and a common space both parties desire, I define conflict as *two or more objects trying to occupy the same space at the same time*.[2]

The "objects" could be persons, groups, or organizations. The space is their interrelatedness, where the interaction of their goals or intentions takes place. For Laura and her friend the space was a cardboard box both wished to occupy. Conflict space can be a piece of territory between two warring nations, or the competing wishes between husband and wife (one wants to use vacation time for golfing and the other wants to go skiing). In each situation conflict occurs over what shall happen, when, where, and how.

In identifying conflict issues it may be helpful to say, "remember the box." Then ask, "Who or what are the two or more objects trying to occupy the box? What is the box they are trying to occupy in this case?" This method allows one to identify the conflicting parties, their competing goals, and the issue around which their interaction is provoked. Only after the conflict has first been defined can one ask, "How do I manage it?"

WHAT IS MANAGEMENT?

Management in general is defined as "the process of seeking to accomplish objectives through the utilization of human and material resources."[3] Management processes are used daily by everyone, from large corporations to individuals who arrange their affairs in order to accomplish their objectives. A church board, for example, may pass a resolution to move the Sunday morning service from the sanctuary to the fellowship hall during the winter in order to save money on fuel. Their pastor, Peter Hansen, is left with implementing the move. He must arrange a configuration of things and people to accomplish the goal of moving the service. He must put the announcement in the bulletin; he must see the maintenance man about arranging for the lectern, chairs, and the piano; he must contact the choir director to see what the choir's requirements for the fellowship hall are; he must contact those responsible for the coffee hour usually held in the fellowship hall after the service to see if they can move to another room. Pastor Hansen may not do all these things himself. His management strategy may be to get others to help him with the details.

This example of management is fairly straightforward. It presumes no major conflict. Yet, conflict is inevitable and ever present in human society. Because this is so, management of conflict must be a part of any general management process. In fact, it is conflict that blocks and hinders the accomplishment of objectives and, unless the conflict is dealt with, the objectives will never be accomplished. Suppose, for example, that early in December some of the council members have second thoughts about moving the service to the fellowship hall to save on fuel. "We have always worshiped in the sanctuary. . . . We can't worship as well anywhere else. . . . It will hurt our attendance," they protest.

"These are just rationalizations," thinks Pastor Hansen. He decides to counter their resistance by forcefully pushing for the move. As a result battle lines are drawn and the issue for the council is shifted to, Do we support the pastor or not?

Hansen makes a serious management mistake. He fails to

focus on that which blocks the organization from achieving its objective of saving fuel—namely, the board's style of decision making and its refusal to take responsibility for its decisions. Rather, he diverts the council to another issue—support the pastor or not—by pushing forcefully for his own preference (moving the service was originally his idea). He may be right in his desire to be ecologically responsible, but he makes a mistake in his management procedure. He forsakes his responsibility to tend the management process in order to push for his own goal.

Conflict could, of course, arise at any other part of the process as well—with the maintenance man, choir director, or those arranging the coffee hour. In each case the conflict must be managed in a constructive manner or the accomplishment of the objective of moving the service could be blocked.

Every organization must manage the conflict that is a natural part of its life. Someone or some group within an organization must take responsibility for establishing and maintaining the conflict management process, otherwise the conflict blocks the organization and the individuals within it from achieving their objectives. The core of this process can be stated simply: (1) identify the issue, the area of concern or conflict; (2) clarify the goals or wants of the various parties; (3) search for alternatives that enable all parties to achieve as many of their goals as possible; and (4) covenant to follow the chosen alternative.

Stating the process is simple. Implementing it is more difficult. Often our human failings get in the way. We avoid the conflict rather than face it. We want our way; we don't care what others want or need. We grow tired of pursuing alternatives that would be best for all and settle for a quick solution. We grow weary of nurturing and tending the process and pursue our own interests. We tire of listening and taking seriously the needs and goals of others.

As a manager in the church, Pastor Hansen has a responsibility first to tend to the conflict management process for the sake of the whole organization and only then to push for his personal goals. If he doesn't, conflict becomes unmanageable and destructive. The organization does not achieve its goals.

The individuals feel frustrated and angry and do not know where to vent that frustration and anger. In this case, because no one tended the conflict management task, the process broke down. Pastor Hansen felt unjustly attacked and unsupported since he thought he was merely advancing the original goal of saving fuel. The council members felt attacked and misunderstood by the pastor. They merely wanted a meaningful and well attended worship service. As a result, neither party emerged from the conflict feeling good about themselves or each other. It became another issue of resentment added to the increasing barriers between pastor and laity.

Before we can fully understand the management of conflict, however, it is necessary to examine the roots of conflict within our own nature as human beings.

THE NATURE OF PERSONS

When I was a youngster of eight, there was a phase of my life in which I imagined that everyone else in my immediate world was acting out the drama of my life. Parents, uncles, aunts, cousins, friends, and teachers would appear, say their parts, and go off stage until their next appearance. I delighted in the fact that everyone took such time and effort just for me. Everything went so smoothly. My own question was, When did they rehearse their parts?

As a child I, like every other child, was merely experiencing the world as centered around me. Maturity taught me that other persons were not staging life just for me, and I came to realize that every person experiences the world as his or her own world. Why? Because all of us see the world through our own perceptual framework or set of glasses. These glasses structure the world for us. They provide categories through which we order and relate our experiences, thus giving meaning to them. Immanuel Kant, in his classic *Critique of Pure Reason*,[4] asserts that the human mind has certain *a priori* or pre-existing categories through which it perceives and understands the world. One can never know, he maintains, "the thing in itself" behind the sense data, and these sense data are formed only through the "given" categories of the mind.

Jean Piaget observes the same framework in persons but calls the categories "schemata." Unlike Kant, Piaget does not regard these schemata as *a priori* or permanent. They develop in order to provide a structure for organizing experience and giving meaning to it. The schemata are usually not conscious, but they are the organizing structures of the mind. As Piaget says, "contacts with experience . . . do not become stabilized until and unless assimilated to structures; these structures need not be innate, nor are they necessarily immutable, but they must be more settled and coherent than the mere grouping with which empirical knowledge begins."[5] Piaget also acknowledges that schemata are modified by experience. A schema will either assimilate a new experience into a familiar structure or modify the structure to accommodate the new experience.

We constantly try to "make sense" out of reality by shaping our experience and interpreting it to fit into the scheme we regard as meaningful. As an eight-year-old, interpreting life as a stage with the drama being played out solely for me made sense for a short time. It soon, however, began to break down. As an adult I continue the search for an interpretation of life and experience that "makes sense" to me. For humans such responses come as naturally as breathing, for we are inevitably "meaning makers." If our capacity to "make sense" is impaired, meaningful human life is diminished.

We are, however, not just passive receivers of experience from the world and shapers of that experience in our minds. We are also actors in that world. As with the schemata of Piaget, human intention is not always conscious to the actor, but it is purposeful. Laura and her friend were not aware of why they wanted to get into the box, but both sensed it was important to them at that moment. Depth psychology, since Freud, has helped us understand the purposefulness and intentional nature of human behavior even when it is unconscious in its origin.[6]

The following diagram presupposes the intentional nature of persons and assumes that they experience their world and act in it from the perspective of their own unique perceptual frameworks. The purpose of the diagram is to identify the components of human action and to serve as the theoretical scaffolding for understanding conflict.

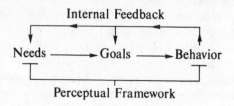

This understanding of human nature presupposes that every person has basic innate *needs*.[7] The activity of one's life seeks to fulfill this set of needs. In order to fulfill these needs, a person works towards *goals*. Goals are states of being that do not now exist but that we can imagine existing. For example, I cannot play the piano but I can imagine myself playing one someday if I take lessons and practice. In other words, goals are targets toward which we direct our actions. These actions are called *behavior*. The diagram shows a goal coming before behavior, even though behavior is the movement towards a goal. The diagram merely illustrates that a goal—something towards which behavior is moving—must be anticipated, though not accomplished, before behavior is activated.

The model also recognizes that persons have an automatic *internal feedback* process that operates at every step of the cycle. When a goal is achieved, internal feedback checks to see if achieving that goal really fulfilled the need or not. At the behavioral level, there is feedback as to whether or not that behavioral pattern really achieved the desired goal.

Whether something satisfies or not can *only* be determined by the individual who experiences it. Had my fatherly intervention with Laura and her friend tried to convince her that sitting in the box was not fun, it would have failed. Laura had already experienced the pleasure involved. The friend's goal of occupying the box threatened her pleasure. With enough parental pressure I could have made Laura feel guilty about sitting in the box and not sharing it. Or, perhaps I could have diverted her attention to something else by making it sound more appealing. Had Laura been offered these various choices she would have decided which, from her perspective, was most satisfying and acted according—even if she had to pay the price of parental and peer disapproval. If she received enough mixed signals from the parent, peer, or herself, whatever choice she made would not have been fully satisfying.

To continue using this episode as a paradigm of human experience: choice of goals and behaviors is not always fully satisfying. The choice of one action as a presumed way out of a conflict may in fact lead to a more dissatisfying conflict. Nevertheless, to be human involves three unavoidable realities: (1) the individual alone makes a choice of goals and behaviors; (2) this choice is made on the basis of what that individual deems is right from his or her perspective at that moment; and (3) the individual determines if the result of this choice satisfies or not.

The diagram shows the movement in linear fashion. Actually, it is more cyclical, constantly moving from felt need, to anticipated fulfillment in a goal, to behavioral pattern towards that goal, to either satisfaction or dissatisfaction that puts one back at the need level again. Persons constantly try to satisfy multiple needs simultaneously and work toward many goals at the same time. One goal may, in fact, satisfy more than one need; one set of behaviors may be designed to accomplish several goals.

ROOTS OF CONFLICT

The roots of human conflict are to be found in the soil of human nature. One root is our intentional, purposeful nature; a second, our perceptual framework determining the choice of goals important to us; a third, our social nature. We are social beings whose goal fulfillment is achieved in an environment that includes other persons. There we also discover the goals of others claiming the space we intend to occupy.

Families illustrate this human condition vividly. Parents have expectations, often quite demanding, of their children. Just as regularly, children have their own notions of what they want to do and be. The issues are often simple, but the conflict wrenching nonetheless. Father comes home from work in the afternoon. The son wants him to pitch baseball, and the daughter wants him to take her shopping. Mother, who has just returned from work herself, wants help in preparing dinner and with other household chores. Father only longs for his easychair, the newspaper, and a chance to enjoy some solitude. Thus, the conflict is born. All are competing for each other's energy and space at the same time. How shall each use his or her energy for the next hour?

CONFLICT: THE INEVITABLE

To be human means you will have conflict. You will experience it within yourself, between yourself and others, and between yourself and organizations. Yet in most of us there seems to be an innate desire for a conflict-free existence. Most of the great religions of the world promise a future pictured as a blissful, peaceful, conflict-free state.[8] Even a majority of social theorists regard conflict as basically dysfunctional and destructive. They are concerned primarily with its reduction or elimination.[9] The church perhaps embodies most vividly this human desire to avoid conflict. The Christian faith is usually interpreted as being opposed to conflict. As a result, most churches develop norms rejecting behavior that encourages conflict and rewarding behavior that tends to suppress it.[10]

We continue, however, to seek our own fulfillment and wholeness. This goal-directed action inevitably encounters and conflicts with other humans' pursuits of their own goals. The only option we have is not *whether,* but *how* to deal with conflict. This book advocates facing conflict directly in order to avert its becoming destructive. Facing conflict openly is also an opportunity for creativity. To be creative means bringing new possibilities into being that presently do not exist. Creative conflict management means creating new alternatives that allow maximum fulfillment for all parties involved. For example, the father, mother, daughter, and son in the earlier illustration could confer, share what each wants, and then design alternatives to best satisfy each of them. The daughter might help her mother with work in the house while the father and son pitch baseball. Then the mother could take her daughter on a brief shopping trip while the father and son complete dinner preparations. After dinner the father would have some solitude to read the newspaper while the daughter and son cleaned the kitchen and washed the dishes. The mother uses this time for her relaxation.

Obviously, every conflict does not work out so satisfactorily. Why? Because we often will not take the time and energy, even when only a small amount is needed, to discover what the conflicting parties want and to explore some alternatives that would enable them to get what they want. Most often we try to avoid the conflict in various ways. The father may use his power and refuse to discuss the issue, storming off to the den, feeling that no one in the family sympathizes with how hard he worked that day. The mother, feeling like a martyr, hardly speaks during dinner. The son pitches the ball against the wall just below the den windows, and the daughter plays loud music. Thus the scene is set for a more angry confrontation in which the original goals will most likely become obscure and the conflict more destructive and unmanageable.

PERSONS, GOALS, AND ORGANIZATIONS

Persons as willful, goal-directed beings cannot achieve their goals in isolation. Organizations are social groups designed to enable persons to accomplish some things together that they could not achieve alone. Organizations obviously vary widely in size, structure, and purpose, from a nuclear family to General Motors.[11] We, as individuals, participate in a variety of organizations for varying periods in pursuit of different goal fulfillments. I, for example, invest myself in a nuclear family, an extended family, a church, a job at a seminary, professional associations, a boys' basketball league, an international agency; and the list goes on. Each one represents for me a setting in which some of my needs are met, some of my goals fulfilled. Some organizational involvements are short-term for me—they prove to be unsatisfying, or I accomplish what I want and move on.

Those organizations that serve a larger segment of the population's goals, such as schools, churches, businesses, or government, become highly institutionalized, while informal organizations, such as short-term groups, are less structured and controlled. Peter Drucker reminds us that "the Lord did not create people as 'resources' for organizations";[12] rather, organizations are created by and for people. An organization does, however, function as a living organism with its own goals, personality, and temperament. In the process an organization often consumes people, turning them into means to its own ends, rather than serving as an instrument for the achievement of their goals. That process inevitably creates conflict.

As we seek the fulfillment of our goals, we search the social stage looking for appropriate settings in which to invest our energies to achieve the goals we perceive will meet our needs. When the organization tries to appropriate us for its own ends, or someone else's wishes prevail over ours in that setting, we are tempted to flee. Yet, we may have no alternative except another organization. A man, for example, may feel his needs are ignored in his family; so he decides to leave. Still, he must seek another human community in which to meet his needs. Often, because he has not learned to manage the conflict in the original family setting, the pattern repeats itself wherever he goes. The same drama is played out for all of us, wherever we turn. The organization makes its demands; we all must pay the rent in some way. Other members compete for the space and resources we want. There is no escaping the drama. The only option is how we respond to it.

MENTAL MODEL: A DETERMINER OF CHOICES

Before we commit or invest energy in a particular setting, we evolve a model or mental picture of that organization. This model represents our perception of that external reality, how it functions, and what the possibilities are for our goal attainment within it.[13] Our mental models are often based on little empirical information. The evidence may be as flimsy as redundant hearsay or fantasy conjecture. On the other hand, they may be based on sound personal experience in that organization. Whichever the case, we—with this image shaping our expectations—act on what we perceive is possible for us in that particular setting.

John Young, for example, graduates from college with a major in communications. He chooses a low-paying job with a major network in New York rather than one at a locally owned radio station because he judges the former as a better route to his ultimate goal of national visibility and a large salary. Disappointment follows. After two years he is still in an obscure job with little hope for advancement. Now he looks at the local radio station as a brighter option. "Perhaps," he thinks, "my goals could be better pursued there." Or, John may even modify his original goals of fame and fortune.

John's story illustrates the continuing process of human experience. We assume a particular organizational setting will be right and fulfilling for us. It isn't! We experience disappointment and conflict so we look somewhere else. Conflict actually helps us in this case. It is a signal that our hopes and expectations are blocked. Either other persons' goals compete with and block ours, or that organization is an inappropriate place for us to achieve our goals. In either case, we must stop and assess. Can we find new ways in that setting to achieve what we want, or must we seek another setting? John finally changes his setting. Yet, conflict awaits him even in the small-town radio station.

Are there any settings, any organizations in which there is an absence of conflict? No, not in this life—perhaps not even in the Kingdom. Why? Remember again the realities of human life suggested earlier: we are intentional, goal-directed beings, seeking the fulfillment of our needs through the achievement of our goals, and we are beings who must pursue our goals in social settings. Other persons are on the same quest in the same settings. Thus, the clash—many trying to occupy the same space at the same time.

THREE TYPES OF GOALS

Another way to understand the dynamic of conflict that confronts us in every organization is through the three types of goals always present and in conflict with each other: personal goals, personal goals for the organization, and the organization's goals.

Persons have goals that have nothing to do with a particular organization of which they are a part. These personal goals may, nevertheless, affect their behavior in that organization.

John Reynolds, an active layman and a member of the church council of First Church, is an avid golfer. On a beautiful spring morning he dutifully comes to Sunday worship, but he sits near the rear door, keeps looking at his watch during the service, hardly speaks to anyone afterward, and wants to skip the coffee hour and rush to the golf course as soon as worship concludes. Until it was announced during the service, John did not know that the pastor had called a special meeting of the church council following the coffee hour. With his tee-off time already arranged with his friends, he makes the quick decision to skip the council meeting. The pastor and some of the other council members are irritated when they learn that John played golf instead of attending the meeting. John's primary goal of playing golf that Sunday has nothing to do with the church, but it influences his behavior in relationship to the church.

All of us experience competing goals continually. We make choices to invest ourselves in one place rather than another. We never fully commit ourselves to one organization. Even when bodily and emotionally present, we never invest one hundred percent of our energy. Other interests and commitments pull us in opposite directions. This reality inevitably creates conflict within us because we cannot do everything and must choose priorities. These choices also cause conflict with others who want us to invest our energies according to their priorities for us. The pastor wanted John at the meeting and was angry when he skipped. The higher the importance of the meeting for the pastor, the greater will be his disappointment and anger over John's absence.

Everyone who is a participant in an organization, however minimally, has personal goals for that organization.

When we invest ourselves in a particular organization, we automatically bring with us certain expectations for the organization. There are things we want to see it do and be. These expectations grow out of our own personal goals and how we perceive they might be fulfilled in this particular setting. Jane Snyder, for example, is a devoted, if not fanatical, tennis player who firmly believes her church should build a couple of tennis courts and start a church tennis league.

"It is a way to get people of all ages involved in church activities," she asserts.

She never misses an occasion, whether it is the church council meeting or an informal gathering, to stress the idea. The church council and the pastor are adamantly opposed to the idea. "Such an activity is inappropriate for a church's ministry," says the chairperson of the council. "To spend money on tennis courts when we have cut our mission giving would be irresponsible and unfaithful."

Jane may have totally unrealistic expectations for what goals are appropriate in the church, but as long as she perceives them as proper, she will work and push for them. Many congregations endure the "enthusiasm" of such members.

On the other hand, there are the so-called apathetic church members. Why won't they get involved? They only attend services occasionally, or not at all. They contribute little to the ongoing life of the church. Therefore, conclude many pastors and lay leaders, these infrequent worshippers have no goals for their church. Such is not the case. Many pastors learn the hard way when they attempt to change something in the parish. Suddenly, a horde of these apathetic members rise up in arms because the pastor has just trespassed on one of their cherished desires for the church. As long as the church continues in ways that these members want to see it go, they may appear apathetic and uninvolved. If the church suddenly starts moving in a direction with which they do not agree, however, they come out of the woodwork. Members who have not attended services for years may show up the day a crucial vote on some controversial measure takes place.

Apathetic and uninvolved behavior can also be a signal that these members have given up on the church. They perceive the church as a setting in which their primary hopes and concerns are not taken seriously, that fulfillment of their cherished hopes has no possibility there. We human beings have an innate wisdom: where our internal sensors for satisfaction tell us there are no fulfillment possibilities, we will not invest ourselves.

At the other extreme, some members find in the church a major setting for gratification. As a result, they invest time, energy, and resources. Their involvement and satisfaction continue as long as they experience fulfillment of their goals. None of us, however, finds complete fulfillment in the church. All of us have other social settings in which we invest our energies to accomplish our life goals. Thomas Luckman, in his book *The Invisible Religion*, points out clearly that people in our society have less need to be visibly religious or to participate in official religious institutions because they have so many other options that enrich their lives.[14] Humans need a source of meaning, a place for goal fulfillment, but resources for meaning are multiple in our culture.

The organization has goals.

These goals determine how the organization spends its energy and resources. These directions may not be clearly articulated in a written set of goal statements; they may be hard to discover by the outside observer or even the regular member. However, like an individual, an organization has a definite set of goals. These priorities, whether clearly articulated or not, direct its actions and energies.

The organizations that receive the highest degree of commitment, energy, and motivation from their members are those whose organizational goals coincide with the goals their members have for the organizations. If an organization begins to alter its goals and move in a direction that differs from a member's personal goals for the organization, then the member's level of involvement, energy, and commitment declines. Apathy, frustration, and anger sometimes result. As folk wisdom suggests, "No one is so apathetic or resentful as when he or she is working on someone else's goals."

Conflict in an organization, whether a local church, a large business, or a family, results in large part from the clashing of these three competing sets of goals—personal goals, personal goals for the organization, and the organization's goals. In a local church, conflict sometimes erupts when the pastor and a small group of lay persons determine the priorities the church will pursue, only to find a large portion of the congregation either turned off or angry about the new direction. Conflict may also be provoked if one person has a special interest, such as Jane Snyder's tennis court, which he or she keeps urging the church to pursue.

Before conflict can be managed effectively, these three competing sets of goals must be identified and satisfied. Satisfaction does not mean the organization has to provide the means for fulfillment for all its members. To be faithful to its mission the church may reject Jane Snyder's desire for a church tennis court. A caring and affirming ministry to Jane, however, requires that she and her goal be taken seriously. Such caring includes helping her to evaluate the importance and appropriateness of her goal and then exploring alternative routes to its achievement.

The purpose of the church is not merely to be the setting in which all human needs are met. To be faithful to its mission requires focus. It means saying no to some human wants and yes to others. Faithfulness demands purposefulness on the part of individual members and the church and the willingness to deal with the conflict that is generated as they search for a common vision.

WHO MANAGES CONFLICT?

Most pastors and lay leaders do not regard themselves as conflict managers. Yet, like it or not, that is one of their chief tasks. Most want to deny, avoid, or perhaps suppress the inevitable conflict that emerges with the clashing of these competing sets of goals. Their aim is to run the church smoothly, let only minimal differences surface, and avoid as many serious confrontations as possible. As a result, much of the conflict in the church is managed in "parking-lot" fashion. Lay persons leave a meeting dissatisfied because their ideas and hopes were not taken seriously or the committee chose a direction they do not support. Rather than raising differences in the meeting or articulating their own hopes forcefully, they complain to friends in the parking lot afterwards. In the security of friendship and the safety of a parking lot they speak boldly of their objections and wishfully of their hopes.

The "parking-lot" phenomenon operates prior to the meeting as well. Some key persons get together and agree on what will be decided before the decision-making meeting is ever held. In short, a small group makes decisions and announces them in some fashion to the remainder of the committee. With the announcement comes a generous dose of persuasion to convince other members to support and work on the goals that have already been selected. Too often in churches, the conflict over priorities is not dealt with openly and publicly. This "parking-lot" policy making results in apathy, alienation, or even hostility among members of the church.

Conflict over contrary hopes, decisions, or priorities does not have to end in alienation or apathy. It can be an occasion for great creativity and growth. The church is a unique institution with a special mission. It can provide the setting in which persons share their deepest needs and hopes and seek growth and wholeness. By engaging clergy and laity together in the exploration of that mission, and by managing the conflict that inevitably arises from the different interpretations of that mission, the church can experience a new creativity and vitality. Growth is not possible, however, unless management processes within the church function to encourage expression of diverse hopes, make the differences visible, and explore alternatives for attaining divergent goals. The pastor, whether effective or not, is the primary manager in the system. For the health and vitality of the church and its members, conflict management must be a pastoral priority.[15]

CONFLICT AVOIDANCE

Pastor Joe Bates's heart began to pound when he walked into the council room and saw Sue Barker slouched in her chair, tears rolling down her cheeks. His immediate impulse was to rush over, give comfort, and ask what was wrong. He resisted and just waited. June Street and Bob Downs were huddled around talking to her. Paul Whiting and three other council members sat with puzzled looks—observing, their lips drawn tight, with some obvious irritation and even anger. Other members were filing in, taking their seats around the circle.

Trying to be calm and collected, using his best conflict management style, Joe Bates finally asked Sue Barker if she would share with the group what was happening with her, suggesting that perhaps together they could work on the issue.

Sue hesitated, sniffed, and then blurted out, "It's the horrible sexist language in this group. Every meeting is drenched with it. The leaders show no sensitivity to the language of the liturgy, the hymns, or the scripture. It is one hundred percent male."

Pastor Bates caught a glimpse of Paul Whiting, who led the service, shifting in his chair, his face growing red with anger. Bates's own anxiety was increasing as he thought how he had worked to get Paul Whiting and some other more conservative members on the council. Criticism of the pastor and "his liberal allies" on the church council had been increasing in the parish. Bringing the divergent factions together on the council where their differences might be aired more directly, Bates hoped, would stem the rising tide of dissatisfaction and behind-the-scenes criticism in the parish.

Paul Whiting was on his feet, glaring at the pastor. "I don't like to get angry," he said, "especially in the church. But obviously some people on this council are more interested in social issues and trivia like language than they are about the gospel. That's what's wrong with this parish. It has deserted the faith for the frivolous." With that he stalked out of the room, casting an inviting glance at his three cohorts.

Pastor Bates, his anxiety now at an all-time high, felt immobilized. He wanted to run after Paul Whiting and convince him to come back. He was angry at Sue Barker for her continual pressing of the feminist issue. He was mentally kicking himself for urging liberal and conservative representation on the church council. Jesus' words from the text earlier in the evening kept ringing in his head: "Love your enemies and pray for your persecutors." But who were his enemies? The thought occurred to him that all the council members were his enemies. At that moment he just wanted to go home.

Declaring that conflict can bring new vitality and creativity is one thing; allowing, encouraging, and enabling it to happen is another. Even Pastor Joe Bates, with his high commitment to dealing with conflict publicly, wanted to flee when the conflict began to threaten his cherished hopes for the parish. Our culture has deeply embedded, at least in the broad American middle class, a desire to avoid conflict. Richard Walton, in his book on managing conflict, points to three primary factors that inhibit persons and organizations in our culture from dealing directly with conflict.[16]

The first inculcated inhibition is to be ashamed of feelings of anger and hostility, viewing them as signs of immaturity or just bad manners. I became clearly aware of this cultural inhibition the day I overheard a grandmother admonishing her grandchild for a fit of anger by saying, "Don't you realize that getting angry destroys your brain cells?" Paul Whiting was angry and felt required to apologize for it, especially in the church, but he could not stay to deal with it. Pastor Bates was angry, but he could not express it. He too wanted to flee to the safety of home. Such an attitude of repression remains in many of us and makes it difficult to express our angry and hostile feelings or to face conflict openly with another party.

The second factor that prevents our dealing openly with conflict is that it requires so much emotional energy. In a serious dispute, emotional involvement goes up dramatically. Repressing conflict requires some emotional energy; facing it openly often demands even more. Pastor Bates was startled by the acute awareness of the emotional cost of conflict. The price suddenly felt too high. He wanted to keep the conflict underground. Like Bates, we often hope to avoid the double bind of acknowledging our angry and hostile feelings and facing the conflict openly.

The third factor is that there are genuine risks in facing a conflict openly. Wounds are opened that are difficult and long in healing. Resentments and antagonisms emerge that may come back to haunt us in some future relationship. The risk increases when the conflict involves another party who has some authority or power over us. Any open conflict with a more powerful party might lead to painful retaliation. Pastor Bates could imagine Paul Whiting and his like-minded conservative friends leaving the church or drastically cutting their pledges. The success of his own ministry seemed to hang in the balance. He just wanted the conflict to go away; if it didn't, his ministry would be threatened.

The power of these inhibiting factors increases even more in the context of the church where the norm is that Christians should love everyone—especially each other. Open conflict is interpreted as unloving and thereby clearly unchristian. It is especially difficult for a pastor, who is seen by many as the role model of a Christian and who, therefore, should not engage in conflict at all. Thus, it is not surprising that we, as products of our culture—particularly within a church context—should find it extraordinarily difficult to face conflict and develop those skills and capacities necessary for dealing with conflict creatively.

CONFLICT: DESTRUCTIVE OR CONSTRUCTIVE?

The option for human beings, however, is not whether to experience conflict or not. The only choice is whether this conflict will be managed constructively or destructively. The evidence is overwhelming that a persistent management style of avoidance or repression of conflict ultimately has a destructive effect on a person, a relationship, or an organization. George Bach, a therapist and marriage counselor, concludes after many years of observing couples destroy each other that to build a solid and lasting marriage couples must learn to fight together. He says, "We've discovered that couples who fight together are couples who stay together—provided they know how to fight properly."[17] He has, in fact, dedicated much of his work to the art of training people to "fight right."

Organizational research reveals that the most effective organizations are ones that develop processes for managing conflict. Rather than suppress conflict, managers of high performance organizations in all environments tend to deal openly with conflict and work with a problem until a resolution is reached that best meets total organizational goals. Instead of using raw power to force one party's compliance or smoothing over the conflict by agreeing to disagree, effective organizations tend to affirm conflict.[18]

Recognition or admission of the presence of conflict, however, is not enough. We need some hope and belief that we can manage it constructively. Believing conflict will destroy our personal relationships and block the achievement of our goals, we tend to avoid it. Psychological research has shown that some tension caused by conflict and uncertainty is a spur to growth and creativity, but only if there is the hope and expectation that a satisfactory way to deal with the dilemma can be found.[19]

Faced with conflict we naturally look for resources that can aid us. One resource is our religious faith. What, then, does the Christian faith have to say about the nature of conflict and its management? The next chapter will focus on that question specifically.

NOTES

1. For a detailed breakdown and analysis of the components of a conflict relationship, see Raymond W. Mack and Richard C. Synder, "The Analysis of Social Conflict—Toward an Overview and Synthesis," *Conflict Resolution: Contributions of the Behavioral Sciences,* ed. Clagett G. Smith (Notre Dame, Ind.: University of Notre Dame Press, 1971), pp. 8–9.

2. Though we come to a similar definition separately, Leas and Kittlaus define conflict in almost the same precise fashion as "two pieces of matter trying to occupy the same space at the same time." Spead Leas and Paul Kittlaus, *Church Fights* (Philadelphia: Westminster Press, 1973), p. 28.

3. M. Gene Newport, *The Tools of Managing* (Reading, Mass.: Addison-Wesley, 1972), p. 2.

   For those interested in pursuing some additional reading in general management theory and practice that does not require extensive background knowledge see:

   (a) Robert R. Blake and Jane S. Mouton, *The Managerial Grid* (Houston, Tex.: Gulf Publishing, 1964). A management approach that seeks a balance between concern for persons and concern for tasks.

   (b) Peter A. Drucker, *The Practice of Management* (New York: Harper & Row, 1954). One of the classics in the field of management. Many others draw from him.

   (c) Rensis Likert, *New Patterns of Management* (New York: McGraw-Hill, 1961). One of the leading advocates of participative management.

   (d) Charles H. Kepner and Benjamin B. Tregoe, *The Rational Manager* (Princeton, N.J.: Kepner-Tregoe, 1965). Advocates problem solving and decision making as the key management functions. Written for managers to make practical applications of their theory.

4. Immanuel Kant, *Critique of Pure Reason,* trans. Norman Kemp Smith (London: Macmillan, 1950).

5. Jean Piaget, *Structuralism* (New York: Basic Books, 1970), p. 51.

6. Sigmund Freud, "Psychopathology of Everyday Life," *The Basic Writings of Sigmund Freud,* trans. and ed. A.A. Brill (New York: Random House, 1938), p. 106.

7. For those interested in exploring theories of human behavior and needs in more depth, some key representatives of widely differing schools of thought are:

   (a) Sigmund Freud, *The Ego and the Id* (New York: Norton, 1962). Freud understands basic needs, centered in the Id, as negative and asocial and needing to be controlled by the individual and society.

   (b) Abraham H. Maslow, *Motivation and Personality* (New York: Harper & Row, 1954). Maslow understands human needs as socially positive. He proposes a hierarchy of needs in terms of a sequence for fulfillment.

   (c) B. F. Skinner, *Science and Human Behavior* (New York: Free Press, 1965). Stresses the importance of the environment, rather than human needs, as controlling human behavior. A classic statement of the behaviorist approach.

8. For a perceptive theological and philosophical analysis of the concept of peace, see John Macquarrie, *The Concept of Peace* (New York: Harper & Row, 1973).

9. Lewis Coser, *The Functions of Social Conflict* (New York: Free Press, 1956), pp. 20–26.

10. James D. Anderson, *To Come Alive* (New York: Harper & Row, 1973), p. 91.

11. For an excellent introductory overview and comparative study of organiza-

tions see David Silverman, *The Theory of Organizations* (New York: Basic Books, 1971).

12. Peter Drucker, *The Effective Executive* (New York: Harper & Row, 1966), p. 33.

13. For a fuller discussion of model as mental picture and its role in the personal and organizational change process see David G. Bowers and Jerome L. Franklin, *Survey-Guided Development I: Data-Based Organizational Change* (LaJolla, Cal.: University Associates, 1977), pp. 6–7.

14. Thomas Luckman, *The Invisible Religion* (New York: Macmillan, 1967).

15. For an excellent discussion of the pastor as manager and shepherd of the system see E. Mansell Pattison, *Pastor and Parish: A Systems Approach* (Philadelphia: Fortress Press, 1977).

16. Richard E. Walton, *Interpersonal Peacemaking: Confrontations and Third Party Consultation* (Reading, Mass.: Addison-Wesley, 1969), p. 3.

17. George R. Bach and Peter Wyden, *The Intimate Enemy* (New York: Avon Books, 1969), p. 17.

18. Gene W. Dalton, Paul R. Lawrence, and Jay W. Lorsch, eds., *Organizational Structure and Design* (Homewood, Ill.: Irwin-Dorsey, 1970), pp. 11–12.

19. Irwing L. Janis and Leon Hann, *Decision Making: A Psychological Analysis of Conflict, Choice, and Commitment* (New York: Free Press, 1977).

CHAPTER 2

Conflict from the
Perspective of Faith

"I hope to God there is peace in the next life; there surely is none here."

Jane Adams, a high-school English teacher in an inner-city school, was exhausted and the clock showed only 7:00 P.M. The dinner dishes were still stacked in the sink. Trying to motivate her own students and putting up with their antics tired her enough. At home she faced her own teenagers. "Have you done your homework? Practiced your music? Remembered to clean your rooms . . . ?" As if her life were not stressful enough, her husband, Ted, announced at the conclusion of dinner that cutbacks at the office threatened his job.

IS IT GOD'S FAULT?

Yes, in one sense it is! God created us as intentional beings (beings with wills) whose natures are social and historical. Life without others and in the absence of institutions is impossible. Human action inevitably is interaction, while institutions of all forms provide the settings for such interaction. Because we are intentional we hope and plan for the future. In pursuit of these hopes we encounter others on their own quests. Conflict results.

The Bible speaks about persons as created in the image of God. The Genesis stories of Creation, the Garden, and the Fall, interpret the image of God as imbuing persons with a will and the freedom to decide, to take action, even to separate themselves from God. Persons are cast into existence with freedom and responsibility. Jane Adams was well aware of the never ending series of choices she made each day. She felt deeply the ceaseless conflict that confronted her. God may have given her a will, freedom, and responsibility, but she wanted escape and peace. When pressed for clarification, however, she admitted that escape was not precisely what she desired.

"I just want Ted's job to be secure, my children to do well in school, my students to work hard and behave," she said. "That would be heaven."

The Christian faith insists that God did not create Jane Adams or anyone else just for an existence of conflict. God created us for fulfillment, for wholeness, for fellowship with God and each other. The literature of faith is full of such expressions, but nowhere more elegantly stated than by St. Augustine: "Thou madest us for Thyself and our heart is restless till it rests in thee."[1] Wholeness is never complete in this life, yet that hope, that quest, draws us onward. Some of the biblical imagery of this state is to know and do God's will perfectly, for in so doing one shall be fulfilled and whole (Deut. 6:1–3; Rom. 12:2).

Jane Adams in her despair did not ask, "What is God's will for me now?" Although she was a faithful church member, the question never occurred to her. God seemed far away. Perhaps God would, she hoped, provide peace someday. In the meantime, it would help if God or someone could make all those other folk act the way she wanted them to act.

DO I NEED THOSE OTHER PEOPLE?

In A.D. 429 Simeon Stylites, a little-known monk, climbed on top of a stone pillar situated east of Antioch. There he remained for thirty years until his death. He devoted himself daily to scripture reading, prayer, and the ascetic life.[2] Simeon obviously survived for thirty years because others provided for his physical needs—food and some clothing. The pillar saints and the desert hermits in the Christian tradition symbolize extreme dedication and self-sacrifice, but they represent as well a world-denying, avoidance stance toward life. Their great gift to the faith has been to remind us of the need for focus, for concentration and harnessing our energies and powers in the life of the Spirit. Their danger is to obscure or make us forget the other pole of the Christian life—expansion, the opening of oneself to the world, to others, to action and interaction, to conflict. *Expansion* and *concentration*, then, are two movements of the Christian life.[3] As parts of a polarity both are necessary. Expansion without concentration risks rootless, mindless action. Concentration without expansion becomes inert, bodiless, world-denying. It is difficult, if not impossible, to do both at once, but, though they often appear at cross-purposes, both are essential and should form a rhythm in life.

Becoming a whole person emerges out of this rhythm. It requires centering, focusing, knowing what we need, want, value, and are called to do and be. Simultaneously, it requires the expression and testing of these capacities in action, the clarifying of them as others respond to, affirm, and resist our actions. We need other people and, in fact, cannot become fully human without them. But having to interact with other persons invariably brings conflict.

THE CHURCH AS A SETTING FOR CONCENTRATION AND EXPANSION

The church is the corporate entity for ministry, an institutional form in which the rhythm of these two poles is sustained. The church and most congregations generally choose the middle road in addressing either pole. Simeon Stylites is hardly the role model for most contemporary Christians. In fact, monasticism has never predominated as the primary pattern for concentration and focusing in the Christian life, though in some traditions it is held up as the ideal. The church often misuses the gift of the monastic model to make laity and clergy alike feel guilty for their lack of dedication. In addition, the church does little to help laity and clergy understand the necessity of concentration and focus in their lives or to train and support them in methods integral to everyday living.[4]

Churches appear to move more easily into expansion, to interaction. Alas, here too, middle-of-the-road is the norm! Interaction becomes cozy fellowship, social niceties, conformity. Expansion that allows us to express who we are, say what we want and how we feel, and that we can count on others to both accept and affirm—but also encounter and resist—is a scarce commodity in churches. Or, if available, it is only in limited quantities. For expansion and interaction to be growth promoting, diversity and conflict are required.

Churches too easily assume that interaction that leads to conflict will destroy community. Much of church life, therefore, represses differences in order to comfort and not disturb the members. It is even widely assumed that a harmonious, friendly church will be more likely to grow than one that has conflict. A currently popular movement, known as "church growth," has almost sanctified the harmonious principle. One of the vital signs of a healthy, growing church is having the membership composed of basically one kind of people. The old saying, "Birds of a feather flock together," is called in "church growth" terminology "the homogeneous unit principle."[5] Its classic expression is found in McGavran's *Understanding Church Growth:* "People like to become Christians without crossing racial, linguistic, or class barriers!"[6] In the final analysis the homogeneous principle cuts down on diversity and creative differences in order to reduce the amount of conflict. The "church growth" movement fails, however, to perceive the heterogeneity that is present in a church membership even when they all speak the same language, are of the same race and class, look alike, dress alike, and talk alike.

Robert Worley's book, *A Gathering of Strangers*, points out that even the most homogeneous local church is filled with diversity of goals and intentions among its people.[7] But the unspoken conspiracy to avoid conflict is so strong that these "look alike but think differently" congregations repress differences and discourage conflict. Churches have difficulty being arenas of expansion and interaction that could provide models and training for people for the rest of life. Most churches do not take seriously enough their own internal life—how they make decisions, communicate, and manage conflict. Too often they are bland way-stations, while the main action in life is elsewhere.

CONFLICT AND THE CHRISTIAN NORM OF LOVE

The accepted norm for a Christian life is love. If conflict is inevitable, even necessary, what is the meaning of the command that Christians should continually strive to act in love? Many church members interpret conflict as the opposite of love. Time and again within a church group experiencing conflict I hear someone admonishing the group, "If we could just be better Christians and love one another, we wouldn't have all this conflict."

I want to challenge the assumption that to love others means having no conflict with them. In fact, loving, caring for others, investing deeply in them, and risking part of ourselves makes our conflicts more intense. The deeper the relationship, the more significant the conflict.

For an understanding of love from the Christian's perspective, one can begin by looking to one of the classic texts (Matt. 5:43–48) in which Jesus is talking about the nature of Christian love.

> You have heard that it was said, "You shall love your neighbor and hate your enemy." But I say to you, Love your enemies and pray for those who persecute you, so that you may be sons of your Father who is in heaven; for he makes his sun rise on the evil and on the good, and sends rain on the just and on the unjust. For if you love those who love you, what reward have you? Do not even the tax collectors do the same? And if you salute only your brethren, what more are you doing than others? Do not even the Gentiles do the same? You therefore must be all-inclusive, as your heavenly Father is all-inclusive.

The Greek word *teleios* is here translated as "all-inclusive," rather than "perfect" as rendered in the Revised Standard Version. *Teleios* means whole, complete, mature—not moral perfection in the sense we often use it. It refers to the early part of the passage, talking about loving others as God loves. Since the character of God's love is all-inclusive of both neighbor and enemy, *teleios* seems more appropriately rendered "all-inclusive."

In this passage Jesus contradicts the normal state of affairs in which you love your neighbor but hate your enemy. He changes the idea radically. "Love your enemies and pray for those who persecute you." Why is this? "So that you may be sons and daughters of your Father who is in heaven." The passage portrays God's love as all-inclusive; he loves all—the just and the unjust, the good and the evil. God intends for us as sons and daughters to love in the same way.

Clearly, loving our neighbors—neighbors meaning those close to us, who support us, who agree with us—is easier than loving our enemies—those against us. But, what does it mean to love another, whether neighbor or enemy? Putting it in the context of that which makes us unique as persons: we are intentional and goal-directed, guided by what is important and fulfilling to us, and we choose our goals and decide their appropriateness from our own unique perspective. First and foremost then, to love another is to affirm the right and the necessity of that person to have goals, to have intentions, and to have a unique perspective. The biblical text asserts that God's love is all-inclusive. God's love affirms all persons, not just those who do God's will. Thus we are not to love only those who agree with us, whose goals and actions we support and regard as right; Christian love means to affirm and support all persons.

Not only are we asked to love our enemies, we also *need* our enemies. Growth towards all-inclusiveness or wholeness is no natural unfolding. It is an arduous, often painful struggle. Often we discover our blind spots and biases only through our enemies. Resistance from others enables us not only to perceive our own limitations and weaknesses, but to gain insight about our identity and intentions. Seen thus, our enemies—if taken seriously—can be a gift set before us by God's grace.

Jesus' own struggle with his messiahship vividly illustrates the point. First his internal conflict, the struggle with the devil and his temptations, later the people's urging him to become a political messiah, and finally the misunderstanding and confusion of his disciples about the nature of his messiahship were all conflicts for him. Through these adversaries, both internal and external, and the options they offered him, Jesus clarified who he was and what was demanded of him.

A supportive, all-embracing love does not eliminate conflict with our neighbors whom we love. Inevitably the neighbors' goals, which we affirm as uniquely theirs, will clash with ours. We will have different perspectives on what is right and appropriate and the just thing to do. Then God's all-embracing love calls each of us to love both ourselves and our neighbor and to affirm not only our own goals but others' as well. Neither we nor our neighbor should expect to be patted on the head by God and others and told, "That's okay. Do anything you want to do." God's love and will both affirm us and stand over against us.

To love others means we must also hold up for them our own intentions, our own hopes—and the goals and intentions of others in the community. Not to lift up this reality for others is not to love and care for them or ourselves.

For any of us to allow our children, our spouse, our neighbor, our friends, or our boss to pursue their goals—to do anything they want in whatever way they want—without our sharing and making known what we want and what from our perspective is right is not to love them or ourselves enough. This reality means that we inevitably have conflict. The very act of loving itself has the dual sides of affirming and confronting, of supporting and critiquing. It is saying no as well as yes. The very act of love itself creates conflict. This dialectical quality of Christian love is inherent in the very nature of God. God both loves us and affirms us in spite of who we are, and at the same time stands over against us—judging us and calling us to account for our intentions and actions.

LOVE AND ANGER

But doesn't conflict provoke anger? Isn't anger unloving and destructive? Jesus again addresses the issue: "You have learned that our forefathers were told, 'Do not commit murder; anyone who commits murder must be brought to judgment.' But what I tell you is this: Anyone who nurses anger against his brother must be brought to judgment" (Matt. 5:21–22). This *New English Bible* translation makes Jesus' thrust clear: not being angry *as such,* but nursing anger, suckling it, feeding and encouraging it, is what Jesus attacks. Paul hits the same theme: "Be angry, but do not sin; do not let the sun go down on your anger, and give no opportunity to the devil" (Eph. 4:26–27). This is one of the commands the church has seldom noticed: *"Be angry!"* We are commanded to own our anger, not repress it, but we are to deal with that anger before sundown and not suckle it along. Nursing anger increases its destructive potential with consequences to our bodies as well as our personal relationships. Unfortunately, too often the church's norm is just the opposite: "If you are angry, don't show it!"

Modern medicine is now beginning to realize the physiological effects of stress and repressed anger and hostility. The body is so designed that stress, followed by a physical reaction such as fighting or fleeing, does little harm. But, as one research team points out:

> The human nervous system is the product of millions of years of evolution. For most of human existence the demands placed on the nervous system were very different from those placed on us by modern civilization. Survival in primitive societies required that humans be capable of immediately identifying a threat and making a quick decision whether to fight or flee. The nervous system is designed for this kind of mobilization: When there is an external threat our bodies are instantly primed (via a change in hormonal balances and nerve outputs) either to fight or flee.
>
> But life in modern society requires that we frequently inhibit our fight-or-flee responses. When a policeman stops you to give you a speeding ticket or when your boss berates your performance, your body is instinctively mobilized by the threat. In these circumstances, however, either "fighting" or "fleeing" would be a socially inappropriate response, so you learn to override your reaction.[8]

When this physiological response to stress is not discharged and continues to accumulate, a chronic stress level builds. This chronic stress plays a significant role in many illnesses, as a growing body of literature points out.[9] How to deal with stress, anger, and hostility in a culture that socially controls or forbids them is not only a physiological but a spiritual issue as well. Wholeness is rooted in the total person, body and spirit. Love as the Christian lifestyle has no option then but to express the full range of human emotions—anger, hostility, joy, gratitude, and jealousy. Love does not exclude anger. Love that is whole can and must express anger.

A RAISE FOR PASTOR PETER WATTS

Pastor Peter Watts, his wife Carol, and many of the laity of St. Matthew's parish were nursing their anger. Last week the parish council, having asked Pastor Watts to leave the room, rejected the pastoral relations committee's recommendation that Pastor Watts be given a salary raise for the coming year. As Pat Donovan had put it, "Our fall financial campaign did not raise as much money as we hoped; our maintenance and utility bills are increasing. We can't promise money we don't have as a raise." Richard Wardlow had added, "With the economy the way it is, most of our people just don't have any extra money to give."

Peter Watts was stunned when he returned to the meeting and learned of the decision, but he said nothing. Carol Watts exploded when Peter told her later that evening. Peter's admonition that ministry meant serving others regardless of what they did was little comfort to her. She did adhere to her husband's request that she not talk about her feelings among the parishioners, but she withdrew from some of the parish activities. Richard Wardlow and other laity felt a little guilty but also resented the pastor's not appearing to hear the reasons for their decision and their own pain. Many of them had gotten no raises, inflation was eating away at their income, and some were even in danger of losing their jobs.

For Peter Watts not to say to the parish council how he was feeling, what he wanted, and what he needed to sustain his family and to feel affirmed in his ministry was in fact not to love the people of St. Matthew's enough. He did not love them enough to risk expressing his anger and disappointment. He also did not love himself enough to affirm his needs over against their interests.

At the same time that loving means affirming one's own needs it also means hearing the needs, hopes, and fears of those who are in opposition to us. Peter Watts needed both to confront and to affirm. Would that he had been able to say in that parish council meeting, "I understand the tightness of money and that you hate to talk about my raise in my presence, but I feel the need to share with you my anger, hurt, and my feelings of being excluded from your council and your concerns. I also want to hear your concerns and your struggles. We are a community that has differences but that is bound together in Christian love. Only as we can face our differences openly can we finally affirm each other and find a way that leads us individually and corporately toward wholeness."

If one individual, whether Peter Watts, Richard Wardlow, or another member, could have spoken out of his or her anger, hurt, or hope, and then been open to the anger and hurt of others, the community might have changed. Others may then have shared and been open. Reconciliation and new birth might have become possible. Money is essential to sustain physical life, but hidden anger and repressed conflict kills not only the body but also the spirit. Where the spirit dies, individuals and communities wither away.

CONFLICT AND THE WORK OF THE HOLY SPIRIT

Our goals get clarified, acted out, evaluated, and reshaped in relationship to and in encounter with God and other persons. Conflict, then, is essential to the development of humanness. Loving God and others not only takes place in the midst of conflict, it affirms that conflict itself. Stated perhaps even more radically, loving God and others is to be in conflict with them. It means to be open and willing to risk making known to them our intentions and at the same time to know, to take seriously, and respond to their hopes. Loving affirms our differences, but it also searches for creative alternatives that are fulfilling and lead to wholeness for all. Ultimately, knowing and doing God's will, that which draws us towards wholeness, comes partly through our conflict with God and other persons. That lifelong encounter enables us to open the curtain upon ourselves, to search for ourselves as God intends us to be, and to know other persons and through this interaction help them become who they were created to be.

Wholeness is for humans as the oak is to the acorn; it is the final form toward which we by nature strive. Wholeness requires human effort, to be sure, but it emerges also as a gift. The unfolding and the movement toward that for which we were created is at every step a gift of grace, an intervention on our behalf, and our response to that grace. This grace may come as affirmation or simple serving of everyday physical needs, such as a mother nurturing her child. It may also come as confrontation or conflict, forcing us to examine ourselves and to be aware and open to the presence and intentions of others. We do not and cannot control that grace. By its very nature, it comes from outside ourselves. We can only respond and interact with it.

If one interprets the action of God's Spirit in the world as an intentional intervention designed to call and move persons toward that wholeness for which they were created, then conflict can be viewed as an intervention of the Holy Spirit that opens up new possibilities for both parties to grow and change. My own dislike of and natural inclination to avoid conflict make me uncomfortable with this statement, but it feels consistent with the reality that conflict is not only inevitable but a growth-promoting part of life. Rather than being destructive, conflict can provide an opportunity for creating new positive possibilities. Without such encounters we would never face who we are, share our intentions, or discover the inappropriateness or appropriateness of our wants. Equally important, we would never have a chance to encounter the goals of others or assist them in testing their reality. How better could one describe the work of God's Spirit in his creation than as creating those moments in history in which unique persons encounter each other and God, and out of this encounter know themselves and each other more deeply. Such moments provide new possibilities, new birth, and new life.

The biblical accounts, moreover, seem to confirm this premise. The biblical record tells the story of God's action in human history. Within this drama, much of which is conflictual in nature, God's intentions are made known. This revelation of God, in fact, comes clear most often in the context of conflict. The prophet Jonah resisted God, fought him, even tried to flee him, finally discovering God's will in facing and doing that which Jonah spurned most—preaching to the people of Ninevah (Jon. 1–4). Jacob's wrestling with the angel was the occasion for the emergence of his new identity as Israel, the father of the twelve tribes of Israel (Gen. 32:24–29). Time and again the prophets of the Old Testament confronted the kings and people with the Word of the Lord. The price for them personally was often high but, within the conflict they created, others were able to hear the Word of the Lord. Jesus' ministry continually created conflict for individuals, his disciples, himself, the people to whom he ministered, and finally the institutions of the day. In each case the conflict was the setting in which revelation occurred, new alternatives were opened, new choices demanded, and new occasions for growth toward wholeness revealed.

CONFLICT AND SIN

Though I have repeatedly stressed that conflict is inevitable, even essential, for human beings, my purpose is not to glorify conflict but to understand the reality of human life in the world. This reality includes conflict that can have its tragic and destructive aspects. Some people are alienated and estranged from themselves, from each other, and from God. They live in a state of willful separation from God and others and, as a result, can and do act unlovingly and destructively toward themselves and each other. The Christian faith has talked about this estrangement and willful separation as sin. What then is the relationship between conflict and sin?

In a recent article two pastoral counselors, Richard C. Richard and Del Olsen, agree that "Christians must ask themselves if conflict per se is a result of man's sinful condition, or if it is a consequence of the basic limitations of being human."[10] They answer their own question by suggesting that a major source of conflict is our differing personal histories, which give rise to differing values and lifestyles. They conclude that, "These differences can hardly be thought of as 'sinful' since they are a result of a sociological process which is different for everyone. Conflicts arising out of these differences, therefore, are a result of the limitations of the human situation."[11]

What then is sinful about conflict? The two respond: "To the extent that our perceptions have been distorted and our basic needs thwarted by selfishness, egocentricity, and prejudice of the human situation, we may say that a person's sinful condition does play a part in conflict situations—and certainly it plays a very definite part when attempts at conflict management are met with selfish and egocentric responses."[12] They conclude, however, that much conflict is simply the result of the finiteness of being human. "We need to recognize that the amount and intensity of conflict and the degree of difficulty in managing it would be considerably lessened had there never been the Fall. We can conclude, then, conflict per se does not have to be considered sinful and thus always thought of as 'bad' experience in the life of the local congregation."[13]

The authors of this article have a noble purpose, a purpose I share: to legitimize conflict in the church. Yet they are caught on the horns of a dilemma that plagues most who want to legitimize conflict by relying on behavioral science explanations and, at the same time, speak to the church about the nature of sin. Conflict, for them, can be primarily explained sociologically as a difference in background and personal characteristics. Conflict is sinful only when persons are selfish or egocentric in their behavior, which is evidently a result of the Fall.

The problem with their position—and it is a widely held one—is that it does not take conflict or sin seriously enough. They recognize conflict as pervasive in the human community but fail to acknowledge that it is always present and does not appear just on certain occasions when individual differences come out. The intensity and degree of conflict obviously vary, but it is present to some degree in every human situation.

Also, to understand sin as being present only when one is acting selfishly or egocentrically is to misunderstand the nature of sin. We always perceive the world from our point of view, and we act on the basis of it. True, one can understand this fact as the natural human condition, but Christian insight into the human condition sees deeper. Human pride, self-glorification, and making personal perceptions absolute ultimately corrupt. The deification or veneration of our own views builds the barriers, creates the separations, and deepens the estrangement from God and others. As Reinhold Niebuhr in his penetrating analysis of the human condition points out, sinful pride works with such deception that we are little aware even of our own pride or self-deception.[14] Furthermore, we, by our own efforts, cannot break free from this captivity.

It is possible, nevertheless, to take conflict and sin seriously as ever present in the human condition, but at the same time to affirm that conflict is manageable and sin is redeemable! The Christian faith acknowledges, as Paul says, that all are under the power of sin (Rom. 3:10), but it also believes that God is actively redeeming persons from that sinful, alienated state (Rom. 5:1–11). Not to take conflict or sin seriously enough subtly tempts one to deny their reality and not work at management of conflict or a response to God's redemptive activity.

The quandary that has always faced Christian theologians here is the danger of making sin inevitable or equal to finite existence.[15] The Genesis story of the Fall tries to walk this tightrope gingerly by placing the responsibility for sin on the first persons, Adam and Eve, in the Garden, who by their own free choice acted selfishly, thus leading to the estrangement and alienation of people from God and, finally, from each other. Conflict should not be equated with sin, but inevitably under the conditions of finite existence, our sinful nature makes conflict potentially destructive and debilitating. As willful beings who are invariably sinful, we can be counted on to see things from our perspective and to pursue our fulfillment through the achievement of our goals. At the same time, however, we also have the capacity to be open to, affirm, and care about the concerns of others.

THE CAPTIVITY OF CAROL WATTS

Carol Watts was experiencing severe conflict. She desired to be free and autonomous, to be able to express herself freely, to do things as she wanted, rather than be forced into the limited role of the pastor's wife. All her goals were being blocked by what she perceived to be the parishioners' expectations of the pastor, his wife, and family. She felt not so much like a kept woman as a captured woman. She had not chosen the ministry—her husband had. She supported him in that choice—in her words, "It's what he ought to do"—yet she still despised having her husband's primary time and energy claimed by the church. Carol had grown up attending church regularly and even chose a church-related college, but she never dreamed she would marry a minister. Some of the old stereotypes of ministers and ministers' wives bothered her, but she thought her love for Peter would surely overcome all of that. Peter had assured her they could work out any problems that arose in the church and that his ministry would not interfere with their family life. Now after three different parish experiences, Carol knew better.

"It happens every time," she stated sadly. "When the chips are down the church will do in the minister and his family. They did it to us in the last parish and now they are doing it to us again here."

Being a pastor's wife cast Carol into a role that created severe conflict for her. This conflict created separation and alienation between her and the parish, between her and the members who had been her friends, even between her and her husband. There were even times when she thought she could not stay with him in the ministry any longer. She did not want to force him out, to make him choose between her and the ministry, but there were days when she felt she could not stand it any longer, that she was losing herself and her sanity in the process. Richard and Olsen, the two psychologists, might say that the conflict here is due to differences in cultural backgrounds and values. There were cultural and value differences in St. Matthew's parish, but these differences are inadequate as an explanation of the tragedy that was happening to Carol and Peter Watts and to the members of St. Matthew's.

In her withdrawal from the parish and her friends, in her lashing out at her husband, Carol, more clearly than anyone else, recognized her own state of estrangement. She even recognized her captivity as due to forces beyond her own control. Carol remarked that she now knew what St. Paul meant when he wrote: "I do not understand my own actions. For I do not do what I want, but I do the very thing I hate. . . . So then it is no longer I that do it, but sin which dwells within me" (Rom. 7:15, 17). Carol had been so hurt by the way this parish and others had treated her and her husband that her only hope for survival and sanity now seemed to be withdrawal. Yet the more she withdrew and distanced herself from the church and her friends, the more she perceived whatever they did with suspicion. Her friends and other members of the parish began to feel the distance too and, in turn, became more suspicious and judgmental of her. They assumed that she cared little about the church or them, and they felt hurt and disconnected from her. The vicious cycle of estrangement grew deeper, with no one seemingly able to break through and reverse the downward spiral.

Peter Watts's own doubts had escalated during the hassle about his salary raise. He still felt called to the ministry and knew it was the right thing for him to do. But his confidence and assurance that the church members would do the right thing in the end had been shaken. He, too, found it hard to believe that they would really support him when the chips were down. Try as he might to keep it from happening, those barriers of separation came between him and some members of the congregation. He was never quite sure that they understood how unaffirmed he felt, how what they did, supposedly for good fiscal reasons, felt like a direct blow at him, his family, and his ministry.

This situation at St. Matthew's demonstrates that where trust, openness, and caring among people erodes, the power of sin corrupts and spreads like an insidious infection in a human community. The fact that the salary raise for the pastor was later restored did little to change the situation for Peter or Carol Watts. The barriers between pastor and people, between Carol Watts and the parishioners, even her friends, and between Carol and Peter were now so high and rigid that no human effort seemed capable of penetrating them.

The laity experienced these same barriers and the same feelings of helplessness in dealing with the minister and his wife. Many of the laity assumed, as Pat Donovan put it, "I guess Pastor Watts will be moving on now." Many times in the past when things didn't go well a pastor moved on or was encouraged by the parish to leave. To most, leaving seemed the best, certainly the easiest, and perhaps "the Christian way" to deal with the conflict. Yet leaving merely says to the pastor and to the congregation alike, "Some conflict is unmanageable and the power of sin that separates and alienates people from each other is, in the final analysis, not redeemable." Whether consciously or not, the people of St. Matthew's acted as if they believed that humans and their communities are condemned to some level of estrangement from each other, so they might as well learn to live with this reality. To hope for anything else, even in the church, would be ultimately disappointing and personally devastating.

CONFLICT AND THE CROSS

The early disciples must have felt some of that same sense of alienation, despair, and hopelessness in the face of Jesus' crucifixion. They staked their greatest hopes and committed and risked themselves in a new community, a new venture, a new lifestyle centered around a message and a promise of the Kingdom as Jesus proclaimed it. Now all was dashed. They, like the members of St. Matthew's, Pastor Peter Watts, and Carol Watts, had to reconcile themselves to that hard reality of life, that feeling of despair that comes when there is no sense of hope or possibility for escape from an alienated and estranged state.

Yet something dramatic happened to that early band of disciples. In their midst appeared the power of the resurrection, demonstrating that even in the midst of the greatest despair and hopelessness, even in the face of the ultimate enemy—death—God's grace is triumphant. The resurrected Christ transformed their despair into hope and a new dynamism for life. They once were dead, now they were alive in a new way. No longer did that power of sin that had captured them, that had alienated them from themselves and each other and from any hope in the future, have power over them.

It *is* possible to manage the conflict that exists between the members of St. Matthew's and their pastor, Peter Watts, and his wife, Carol. It *is* possible to manage the conflict between Carol and Peter, and even among the laity themselves. It *is* possible to help them get clear what their goals and intentions are, to share these with each other, and to develop some alternatives that are satisfying to all of them. What is not possible, however, is to eliminate all of the conflict in that parish or in the Watts family. It is not possible for them by their own efforts to keep these inevitable conflicts from erecting barriers between them or to prevent alienation and separation from becoming a reality in their lives.

Sometimes even their best efforts only increase the distance between them. Peter Watts's own mild attempt to be more open with the laity was threatening to some. His later sharing of his disappointment with the parish council forced them to deal with issues they would rather have avoided and, thus, pushed them further away. His own attempt to discuss the situation with his wife only reminded her again of how she resented his being in the ministry and what it was doing to her and their family.

In the final analysis, breaking free of this kind of entrapment requires not an act of will but a new perspective. It demands that people perceive the reality of their situation from a different point of view. In more traditional theological language, it requires a conversion, a new way of seeing, a turning around.

Only as our perception, our point of view, is changed can we see all things in a new way. Only then can the laity's nosing into the affairs of the Watts family be seen as their fumbling attempt to be caring and supportive of the pastor and his family. Only by seeing through different spectacles could the laity understand Peter and Carol Watts's hurt. Only from a new viewpoint could the laity of St. Matthew's understand that Peter Watts's pushing them to deal openly with their differences is a way to love and trust each other more profoundly and to feel deeper bonds of caring and support than they had known before.

The testimony of the Christian community throughout its history has been that conversion, that perceiving in a new way, comes as a gift of God's grace and not merely as an act of will. Grace may break in through the words or actions of another person, or through our own private reflections. It may come suddenly or emerge gradually. Or, as Willa Cather put it, "The miracles of the Church seem to me to rest not so much upon faces or voices or healing power coming suddenly near to us from afar off, but upon our perceptions being made finer, so that for a moment our eyes can see and ears hear what is there about us always."[16]

As with those early disciples such a conversion, prompted by God's grace, comes as a new view of reality that has hope rather than despair, that has freedom rather than bondage. The central realities of the Christian faith—the cross and the resurrection—are a testimony to the fact that in the final analysis the power of God's love can overcome even the greatest sense of despair, hopelessness, and alienation. It creates a new reality and enables us to see all things new. This new reality does not eliminate conflict. Conflict is a fact of existence. It does, however, offer a new perspective in which differences are seen not as destructive but as creative possibilities. Conflict is seen not as debilitating but as an opportunity for growth. Conflict is perceived not as an occasion for alienation but new openness to each other. It promises that all things are possible through God's grace.

NOTES

1. *The Confessions of St. Augustine*, trans. E. P. Pusey (New York: Dutton, 1951), p. 1.
2. Williston Walker, *A History of the Christian Church* (New York: Scribner, 1954), p. 137.
3. These two concepts of the polarity were suggested by Rachel Hosmer and Alan Jones, *Living in the Spirit* (New York: Seabury Press, 1979), pp. 149–151.
4. Recently a number of helpful books addressing this issue have appeared. Two written for laity and clergy are James C. Fenhagen, *More Than Wanderers* (New York: Seabury Press, 1978) and Tilden Edwards, *Living Simply Through the Day* (New York: Paulist Press, 1977).
5. C. Peter Wagner, *Your Church Can Grow* (Glendale, Cal.: Regal Books, 1976), p. 110.
6. Donald McGavran, *Understanding Church Growth* (Grand Rapids, Mich.: Eerdmans, 1970), p. 198.
7. Robert Worley, *A Gathering of Strangers* (Philadelphia: Westminster Press, 1976), p. 11.
8. O. Carl Simonton, Stephanie Matthews-Simonton, and James Creighton, *Getting Well Again* (Los Angeles: J. P. Tarcher, 1978), p. 48.
9. For those who want to explore this area further, see K. R. Pelletier, *Mind as Healer, Mind as Slayer* (New York: Delta Books, 1977).
10. Robert C. Richard and Del Olsen, "Go to Your Corners and Come Out Fighting! The Psychologist as Conflict Manager," *Theology News and Notes* (October, 1976), p. 7.
11. Ibid.
12. Ibid.
13. Ibid.
14. Reinhold Niebuhr, *The Nature and Destiny of Man*, vol. 1 (New York: Scribner, 1941), pp. 206–207.
15. Paul Tillich has a good analysis of this dilemma for Christian theology in his *Systematic Theology*, vol. 2 (Chicago: University of Chicago Press, 1957), pp. 39–44. Tillich's own position comes close to equating a person's sinful state with finitude.
16. Willa Cather, *Death Comes for the Archbishop* (New York: Random House (Vintage Books), 1971), p. 50.

CHAPTER 3

Principles for Conflict Management

A longtime friend who introduced me to some principles of conflict management[1] uses an illustration to describe the process. He says that becoming an effective manager of conflict is similar to becoming an artist. The artist must first learn to mix paints, then come to understand which mixtures produce which colors, and, finally, learn brush strokes for applying the paint to the canvas. Only after the artist masters the paint mixing and fundamental strokes does he or she become free from the basic mechanics. Persons who become artists in creative conflict management also must first master the basics and so integrate them into their attitudes and actions that they are able to use them creatively in a variety of conflict situations.

E. B. White, analyzing style in writing, offers another analogy.

> There is no satisfactory explanation of style, no infallible guide to good writing, no assurance that a person who thinks clearly will be able to write clearly, no key that unlocks the door, no inflexible rule by which the young writer shapes his course. He will often find himself steering by stars that are disturbingly in motion.
>
> The preceding chapters contain instructions drawn from established English usage; this one contains advice drawn from a writer's experience of writing. Since the book is a rule book, the cautionary remarks, these subtly dangerous hints, are presented in the form of rules, but they are, in essence, mere gentle reminders; they state what most of us know and at times forget.[2]

The following set of principles, which have evolved through years of working and struggling to learn and teach how to manage conflict, are the paints, brushes, and canvas of the conflict management artist. But, like E. B. White's rules for writing, they are intended as guidelines, stating what most of us know but often ignore. There is no magic formula, no clear roadmap, no master blueprint that automatically applies to all conflict situations. Each conflict has its unique dimensions and its universal qualities. Each conflict has its own actors (at least two), relationships, and goals. The issues come and go. The intensity fluctuates. The potential for either growth or destructiveness is always present.

Most of us know or can learn the guiding principles relatively quickly; they often appear simple or obvious. Yet knowing the rules or having read them is no guarantee of success. The key is being able to use them in those moments when rationality deserts us, when reflection and planning time are nonexistent, when the stakes are high, when our anxiety is intense. Internalizing the principles to become the artist is the goal. Individuals and organizations *can* increase their capacity and skill in managing conflict, but the growth of this talent rarely occurs dramatically or rapidly. Usually it comes slowly; it develops through use.

Let me here offer two suggestions for using the principles of conflict management that follow. First, practice one principle at a time. With the prospect of positive results from conflict situations, perhaps for the first time, most of us desire to be proficient at good conflict management with the snap of our fingers. In fact, such wishful thinking is usually counterproductive. Patterns do not change quickly. If we attempt too much too soon, we fall back into the less successful patterns of dealing with conflict that have become ingrained over many years. However, by focusing on one principle at a time—for example, trying to communicate well—new patterns can be established.

Second, in the beginning try to remember the principles in actual conflict situations. Rarely do we plan when we shall engage in conflict. Suddenly we find ourselves immersed in it. All our best intentions fly out the window. In those moments the principles can be used almost as a checklist, a reminder of things that work. "Have I remembered to . . . ?" Like E. B. White's rules of grammar, we not only need to drill on them in practice sessions but to remind ourselves to use them in the midst of composition as well. Internalizing them so that we freely use them as the artist is the goal, but at the early stages of change even a mechanical reminder system may be necessary.

In this spirit I commend these principles of managing conflict to you. Use them to manage conflict more creatively and constructively. The principles can benefit not only you but the other parties with whom you are in conflict as well.

The adjective *creative* will be attached to conflict management repeatedly in these pages. It intends to point to a style of conflict management that is constructive rather than destructive to persons and groups. The constructive style builds energy while a destructive pattern saps it.

Creative means having the ability or power to create. To create is to bring into being something that does not now exist. Creative conflict management, then, means forging new relational possibilities, new alternatives for action that presently do not exist and that are satisfying to both parties. The goal of creative conflict management is to enable both parties to achieve what is vital and important to them. The principles are intended as guidelines to that end.

1. HELP OTHERS FEEL BETTER ABOUT THEMSELVES

Persons and organizations manage conflict best when they are feeling good about themselves.

Some years ago a group working for the W. Clement and Jessie V. Stone Foundation coined the term *psychological powerbase* to refer to those feelings of positive regard that humans can have for themselves.[3] The word "powerbase" was chosen because it was a more dynamic concept than "ego strength" or "feelings of adequacy." Having a positive regard for oneself was recognized as one of the essential ingredients for healthy human beings who can manage conflict constructively and creatively.

Who has not experienced the effect of feeling bad about himself or herself? A decline in our psychological powerbase triggers several psychological and physiological reactions. Our perceptual frames begin to close in. We become more narrow in our vision, in what we can hear or perceive, and in what we are willing to accept into ourselves. At the same time, we have less energy to act in the world, less confidence that what we do and say makes any difference, less belief that we can achieve our chosen goals.

On the other hand, when our psychological powerbase increases, when we regard ourselves more positively, our perceptual frames open up. We begin to see more options for ourselves. More alternatives are perceived and we have more energy to work on these alternatives. We also hear and are more open to other people's needs and goals and can more easily affirm their validity. At the same time, we are more able to state our opposition to goals of others when they are counter to our own.

All of us have occasions in which we feel put down and less valuable than others, whether these feelings correspond with reality or not. Those brilliant words that come to us later we could not remember while on the scene. In retrospect, every statement seems more fumbling and uncertain than the one before, and our powerbase goes down even further. At other times, when we are feeling good about ourselves or are in a setting in which we feel affirmed, conversation flows. Good ideas emerge readily. Listening to others comes easily. We are open, accepting, and not threatened by the ideas and actions of others.

When our psychological powerbase is low, we are poor managers of conflict. We see fewer alternatives for ourselves. We are less open to the needs of others and more defensive and hostile to the other party. Our natural inclination is to fight, to get the other party, to put others down. In attacking another person, we often lower their powerbase, make them feel worse about themselves, put them on the defensive. They, consequently, become less able to respond openly, nondefensively, and to perceive creative alternatives.

Upon encountering a conflict, if you can first ask, ironical as it may seem, "How can I help other persons to feel better about themselves?" rather than "How can I get them?" the results will often be amazing. This is the first rule for creative conflict management.

Once, a pastor in great distress finally went to a colleague and recounted a long-standing conflict he had with a layperson in his congregation. The layperson was on the church board and seemed always to be on the opposite side of every issue from the pastor. The pastor was at his wits' end.

"What do you think you will do about it?" the friend inquired.

"My primary strategy," he replied, "is to convince the nominating committee not to put this man back on the church board again. That way, I will not have to deal with his opposition at every point. He never thinks I have a good idea."

"Do you ever think he has a good idea?" the friend asked.

"Well no, I don't," he replied somewhat surprised by the question.

After the conversation the two agreed on a different strategy in which the pastor would focus first on affirming the layperson and building his psychological powerbase. He did so in two simple ways. First, whenever he had an idea he wanted to check out with the laypersons in the congregation, he always sought the advice and counsel of that particular person first. Second, whenever that person presented an idea in the board meeting, the pastor made sure the idea was heard, clarified, and affirmed. The change in their relationship came slowly, but it did come.

Such a strategy may sound manipulative; in a sense, it is. Yet, when the intent is sincere rather than manipulative, the other party usually senses it.

WAYS OF AFFIRMING PEOPLE

Affirmation is a key stimulus for positive human development. It nourishes and releases the energy for creative action. Without it persons harden, grow rigid, resentful, and hostile.

Yet affirmation must come as a gift. Even the capacity to affirm ourselves is rooted in affirmation by others. Everyday life provides opportunities for affirmation in small and commonplace ways. Three key ways we can affirm others are:

Listen to another person. As simple as this may seem, few experiences affirm persons more directly or deeply. Carl Rogers, pointing to the healing power of in-depth listening, constructed a theory and practice of psychotherapy around this particular insight.[4] Anxious to be noticed and heard, assuming our utterances will carry the day, most of us invest in our own words rather than the words of others. Mistakenly we assume that speaking rather than listening is the key to being heard.

Take seriously the goals of others as significant to them. To "take seriously" does not necessarily mean to agree. In fact, disagreement may be your final response, but accepting and acknowledging their goals affirms and supports. The ability to affirm but differ is a crucial skill in conflict management.

Look for and appreciate the strengths and gifts of others. Given two sheets of paper and asked to list our strengths on one and our weaknesses on the other, most of us will fill the weakness sheet first. Humility is a desirable trait but obsession with weakness is debilitating. A gift that frees and helps is to focus persons on their assets. This does not mean that we should whitewash or overlook others' liabilities and weaknesses, but we should focus first on their strengths and gifts and affirm them. Feeling affirmed, persons are more able to explore their own weaknesses and failures and work on them.

These three essential ways of building the powerbase of another are simple, but they work. And they can be learned and practiced. The artist of human growth and conflict management cannot do without the three essential tools of listening, taking seriously the goals of others, and focusing on strengths.

Organizations, as well as individuals, have psychological powerbases. A local church, for example, can be so down on itself, believing it has insufficient resources for ministry, that its eyes are blind to the many resources present in its people. Most organizations have more resources than they use. Their primary difficulties are in the areas of discovery and affirmation.

A church with a low psychological powerbase has a lower capacity for managing conflict. Its primary strategy becomes: keep conflict out of sight and out of mind, because it is too threatening. It fears that conflict will destroy its community, that it has no capacity for dealing with conflict once it surfaces. Its only alternative appears to be suppression. Consequently, when approaching a church or any group in conflict, we find one of the first steps is focusing them on their gifts, those things they are already doing well, rather than on the conflict itself. Only after they feel more positive about themselves can they openly deal with conflict. Only then can they adequately perceive their resources and develop creative alternatives for managing the conflict. They may even grow to the point of encouraging open conflict within the church.

PERSONAL POWERBASE – NOT POSITION POWER

Walt Johnson had been president of Burgis Milling Company for only three years, though it seemed longer than that to most employees. A man of sharp intelligence and drive, he had scrambled his way to the top. He prided himself on being a man of decisive action. The company had rarely witnessed three more action-packed years. Reorganization, half the management force turned over—no one doubted that Walt was boss. He tolerated little disagreement within the ranks and none with his decisions. He demanded and received productivity from the employees, or they were fired.

Walt Johnson had plenty of position power, but those who worked *for* him—no one worked *with* him—suspected that underneath the hard-driving exterior hid an insecure, frightened man. Position power did not increase his psychological powerbase. Rather, it covered his feelings of inadequacy. As long as he could be busy and in command he did not feel vulnerable to others and himself.

Position power tempts and entices us with the promise of security and self-assurance. A personal powerbase, feeling good about oneself, has roots in other soil. It remains a distinctly different thing from position power. Personal well-being, the ground out of which the artist of creative conflict management emerges, comes as a gift and a risk. The Christian faith points to both. The gift, essential to humanity, is God's creation and love, not because of who people are or what they do, but because they are God's. The risk is contained in the paradox, "He who gives himself finds himself." He who is vulnerable to others, open to their needs, and not out to control them, he who can give power away, mysteriously receives personal power.

2. STRIVE FOR EFFECTIVE COMMUNICATION

Effective communication consists of in-depth and reflective listening and sending with the knowledge that one's perceptions and messages are uniquely one's own.

It is no secret that an essential ingredient in creative conflict management is the quality of communication among the parties. More has been written on this principle than any of the others. Thomas Gordon, for example, has developed a theory and technique of training persons to be effective parents primarily through teaching them how to become more effective communicators.[5] Self-evident as it may seem, we need to be reminded over and over again of the importance and crucialness of good communication in the management of conflict. It is a skill that can be learned. We can become better communicators with effort.

What do we need to know—or remember, that is—about communication? First, remember the primary fact that there are two parts to communication—the *sending* of messages and the *receiving* of messages. But what a difference it makes in how we send and how we receive messages!

Despite our penchant for sending, the more important part of the communication process is the receiving of the message. More distortion and misunderstanding occur on the receiver's end than on the sender's. Therefore, hearing what the other party is trying to communicate is absolutely crucial. Two ways to do this are in-depth listening and reflective listening. In-depth listening is listening on all levels—both verbal and non-verbal—for messages that come across in another person's communication. While listening to the words, we must also be aware of body signals, tone, emphasis, and the feelings behind the words.

Reflective listening is a method developed by Carl Rogers for his client-centered therapy. It consists of reflecting back to the sender the message we believe he or she is sending. No one receives a message precisely as it is sent. To guard against our distorting or misunderstanding the message we should occasionally check what we are hearing with the sender. This listening process has, of course, spawned its share of humor. The client says, "It's a beautiful day today." The therapist, a new convert into the client-centered method, responds, "I think you said, it's a beautiful day today, didn't you?" While we need not take the process quite so literally and become such repetitive reflectors, validating the message with the sender from time to time helps us remain attentive in an attempt to correctly hear and understand what it is the person is trying to say.

The other side of the communication process is the sending of messages. The most important fact to remember in developing the skill of sending messages is that the message you send is not a statement about an "absolute fact"—it is your perception of the fact. Since each of us perceives the world in our way, the messages we send about our experience will always be from our particular perceptual points of view. In conflict situations our tendency is to become more dogmatic and authoritarian in the messages we send, acting as if we have the final word about the facts of the case. Acknowledging the fact that the message we sent is always our own perception is to admit that we could be wrong. It also recognizes that the other party might have perceptions of the situation that could be as "right" as our own.

COMMUNICATION TRAINING

A little bit of training in communication goes a long way. It can rather quickly boost the effectiveness of individuals and groups in managing their conflicts. An example of a simple training procedure is a three-person exercise used to practice sending and receiving messages. Two people enter into a conversation on a given topic; the third is the observer. The ground

rules are simple: before sending a new message, one must reflect back what he or she hears the other party saying and each
message must be prefaced by an acknowledgment that the message is a relative perception of the situation, not an absolute
fact. The exercise feels mechanical at first, but the process im-
presses upon participants the method of sending and receiving
essential to successful communication.

After conversing for a short period, the two stop and the
observer gives them feedback about how he or she perceived
them communicating. Were they listening well and checking
out what they heard? Were they sending messages that acknowledged the relativity of their perceptions? Usually the observer obligingly shares his or her observations, neither giving a
short summary of the conversation (reflective listening) nor acknowledging the perceptual relativity of the observations! The
trainer can point out this fact, which provides a humorous but
important illustration of the fact that we very quickly fall back
into our old patterns of communication—namely, not listening
and not acknowledging the messages we are sending as our
perceptions.

Becoming an effective communicator, like becoming an artist, requires discipline and practice, but good communication
skills can be learned and used effectively. Communication
styles become grooved patterns, but they need tending to see
that the good ones remain in the groove and improve the less
effective ones.

COMMUNICATION AND THE SYSTEM

The communication style of a person does not affect just that
individual or the one with whom he or she is communicating. It
has an impact on the larger system of which the person is a
part.

Charles White and Everett Stansky, for example, have been
pillars of their church for twenty years. Each has served on
every committee in the church. Charlie usually chairs the finance committee, while Everett runs the property committee.
Consequently, both are on the official board where overall poli-

cy and final decisions are made. Small congregations such as theirs depend on a few of the faithful to sail the ship.

Charlie and Everett play an interesting game with each other. They spar verbally, often boisterously, with each other over most issues that come before the official board. They conclude, however, by supporting the same issues; usually one of them will make the motion and the other will second it. Their communication style leaves little oxygen in the air to sustain the input of other members, however. The minister, meanwhile, feels frustrated and helpless.

One evening the church was blessed with an unexpected gift from soft-spoken Evelyn Baker, a newcomer to the church whose willingness to work quickly landed her on the official board.

"Charlie and Everett, why are you two always angry with each other?" she blurted out in the midst of one of their verbal jabbing sessions. Both looked as if they had been hit in the face with a wet towel.

"Angry?" they responded simultaneously. After another thirty seconds of stunned silence and the exchange of puzzled looks between the two, Charlie said, "Evelyn, you are new here and don't know us. No two people in this church love and respect each other more than Everett and I do."

"Well, you surely have a funny way of showing it," retorted Evelyn. "It seems to me that everyone else here is afraid to speak for fear of getting caught in your crossfire."

"That's right, Charlie," added Betty Rath. "I know you two mean well but you don't realize what you are doing to the rest of us and this church by monopolizing the meetings."

Charlie and Everett, without knowing or perhaps admitting it to themselves, completely dominated the church board by their manner of communicating. The message others heard was, "Your words are of little value. You have no power to influence decisions about the church." The other laity, even the pastor, heard this message. Their behavior told the message had been received—they became passive observers of the dominant duo.

Charlie and Everett also heard the message that evening.

The sting of revelation brought insight and judgment to them. The moment of revelation, however, opened new possibilities not only for the two men but the church as well. If they could alter their style of communication between themselves and with the other members, the climate of the official board meetings might radically change. Correspondingly the actions and interactions of the other members might be different.

To change our communication style is difficult for any of us. Charlie and Everett were no exceptions. But the moment of transformation was at hand. They needed support, knowledge of a new style, and encouragement to pursue it. The system itself, in this case the church council, can facilitate that change. The momentum can come from any part of the system. Perhaps another lay person could respond, "Seems we could all be better communicators. Why don't we work on that as a council."

The unexpected moment of grace, the unpredicatability of the Spirit's intervention, and the possibilities of transformation ever present can all be blocked or opened by the way we communicate.

3. EXAMINE AND FILTER ASSUMPTIONS

Unexamined assumptions contribute to destructive conflict.

St. Mary's Roman Catholic Church was one of ten parishes from the diocese selected to experiment with a new model of team ministry. The pastor, a man of twenty-five years' experience, and his associate, ordained for ten years, were joined by four sisters who ran the parish school. Their mandate was to plan and coordinate the total ministry of the parish as a team, trying to use the resources of each person to the fullest advantage. As part of the pilot experiment the diocese provided a consultant to meet with the team at least twice a month, or more often if needed.

Conflict was not long in surfacing. The stresses and strains of developing a team ministry, which demanded new styles and new behaviors for the pastor, his young associate, and the sisters (who had traditionally played a secondary role in the actual parish ministry) was hard enough. In addition, the sister who was principal of the school was an aggressive, outspoken person. The pastor wanted peace at any price and would do almost anything to avoid open confrontation. The sister confronted the pastor increasingly often at meetings. He responded by fleeing the scene, psychologically or even physically in some cases. He began coming late to team meetings, being sick, or not showing at all. It became increasingly difficult to get the sister and the pastor to the same meeting.

Finally, at a team meeting with the consultant, both were present. The consultant began by reflecting that the pastor and principal seemed to be acting on some assumptions about each other that they never bothered to check out. He asked if they would be willing to write their assumptions down on newsprint. After recovering from the initial shock, both, with some reluctance, agreed. When they finished the task, the two pieces of newsprint were hung on the wall.

The two lists looked something like this:

Principal's Assumptions About the Pastor	*Pastor's Assumptions About the Principal*
• He is not very interested in the parish school, since he rarely visits the school.	• She doesn't want me in her school. I have learned to stay away.
• He is uninterested in teaching even a religion class in the school.	• She doesn't want me to teach in the school, though I would like to teach a religion class.
• I would like to be more involved in the ministry of the parish outside the school, but the pastor won't allow me in his arena.	• She is interested only in the school and cares little for the other parts of the parish's ministry.
• He sees me as a traditional nun.	• She thinks I am a traditional priest, inflexible and unchangeable.
• Deep down he doesn't like me.	• She basically does not like me.

Obviously, every conflict situation is not as dramatic nor the assumptions as vividly contrasted as in this case. Yet in every conflict the participants make assumptions that have no basis in reality but that determine their actions and their perceptions of other people's behavior in the situation. The opportunity to list these assumptions openly on newsprint is not usually possible nor always desirable. To manage conflict effectively, however, some means must be found to make assumptions public and to eliminate, or at least keep people from acting on, those that have no basis in fact or are destructive.

"Judge not, that you be not judged. For with the judgment you pronounce you will be judged, and the measure you give will be the measure you get" (Matt. 7:1–2). Jesus' teaching recognizes that human judgment comes from a personal perspective. That perspective is often distorted by assumptions that may be false and even destructive to the judger and to the one being judged. To project judgment onto another provokes a counter-judgment, which may be as untrue as the original one.

The sister and the priest not only made false judgments of each other based on their unexamined assumptions, but they acted on them. These judgments embodied in action seemed to confirm what the other suspected. The results were a widening of the distance between them and increased suspicion, which led to further false assumptions and consequent reaction. The spiral of alienation thus grew because neither he nor she was free from a judgmental stance toward the other. Only when they were able to share their assumptions and judgments of each other were they able to break the spiral of alienation.

4. IDENTIFY GOALS, WHAT IS WANTED

Identifying what a person, group, or organization is trying to accomplish, what is wanted, in a situation is an essential element in conflict management.

The existence of a conflict means that there are two or more persons' intentions trying to occupy the same space at the same time. Until one identifies what each party wants or is trying to accomplish, in short, what their goals are, one can never manage the conflict.

"How do I survive in conflict?" "How do I keep from being overwhelmed in a conflict?" Repeatedly the threat of conflict and its destructive possibilities flood our minds with such questions. The answer can be stated simply: know what you want, affirm it, and work for it. At the same time be open to hearing and affirming what the other party wants. But, like most tasks in conflict management, these are easier said than done.

Through a misinterpretation of Christian humility and self-sacrifice, many church members have great difficulty saying and affirming what they want. They forget that we are intentional beings who try to accomplish goals we think are important. If individuals had no goals, there would be no conflict. Creative conflict management requires asking again and again, *"What am I trying to accomplish and what is the other party trying to accomplish that has led us into this conflict situation?"*

ASK "WHAT," NOT "WHY" QUESTIONS

"Johnny, why didn't you take out the trash this morning as I asked you? You also have been leaving your bed unmade; how come? And one more thing, your school counselor called to tell me you have not been bringing in your homework. Why have you been telling me you have no homework every night?"

Johnny Calloway sat staring at the floor as his father's questions bombarded him. "I'm sorry. I'll try to do better," he replied when the questions let up.

"Excuses are all I ever get from you. Why not some action?" responded his exasperated father.

What parent has not stood in Bill Calloway's shoes, wondering how to manage the conflict with his child? Parents have so much invested in their children, so many goals for their children's lives, so many things they want them to do and be. Johnny's performance appears to threaten or block all those hopes. Frustrated, disappointed, and angry, the parent seeks an explanation. Why?

Who has not been on the receiving end of "why" questions? How does it make you feel? Apologetic and promising to do better, like Johnny? Or, do you feel judged, resentful, and angry at the accuser?

"Why" questions are rarely experienced positively by the receiver. They tend to have a judgmental and accusing quality to them. They put the receiver on the defensive and provoke either a fight or flee response. Yet in a conflict the urge to ask the "why" question, to accuse, to seek an explanation to behavior with which we disagree is almost irresistible. Perhaps it is the analytical, psychologically oriented culture in which we live. Or, perhaps it is the tip of our prideful nature desiring to keep others in their place and control them to our ends. Whatever the reason, "why" questions have an adverse effect in conflict management. The feeling they communicate is blame. Their direction is the past. They close off the search for alternatives and reduce energy for creativity.

"What" questions, on the other hand, tend to be heard positively. They feel affirming. They are future oriented. "What" questions—"What are your goals?" "What is important to you?"—seem more objective, but whether they are or not, their affirmative tone enables the hearer to relax, to explore his or her desires and hopes, and also to search for new directions without shutting off creativity and energy. "What" questions and "why" questions do not have to use the words what and why, however. They are actually two types of questions, different approaches to interacting with other persons and for managing conflict—one open and affirming, the other judgmental and threatening.

How can Bill Calloway, as a caring and responsible father, get into a "what" stance with his son? That, in fact, is the question we must ask in whatever relationship or conflict we find ourselves. For instance, Bill Calloway could first share his own goals and then ask about Johnny's.

"Johnny, I want you to build your skills now so that you will have more choices and the freedom to exercise them in later life. But, Johnny, I also want to hear what you think is important."

Johnny may not be able to say clearly what he wants, what is important to him, or what he wants to invest himself in right now. Children or adults, all human beings struggle with precisely the same question. That is life's question. We can, however, seek its answer better in an atmosphere that affirms us, that takes seriously what we want, what is important to us, than in an atmosphere that sets us on the defensive, accuses us, or puts down our goals.

Conflict is also our ally in our quest to clarify what our goals are, what is important to us. Being blocked, experiencing resistance can be an occasion to discover where we are trying to go and what we are trying to achieve. Having some person or organization oppose us forces us to examine what is important, as well as makes us hear what the other party wants.

Explore the different ways you ask "why" questions in conflict. Try instead shifting stances and asking "what" questions of yourself and the other party. Nothing will change the way you function in conflict more dramatically.

5. IDENTIFY THE PRIMARY ISSUE

Until the primary issue has been identified and acknowledged by the principal parties in the conflict, it is difficult to manage the conflict.

The council meeting of Birch Road Baptist Church dragged into its third hour. Everyone was anxious to go home. Still no decision on whether to fire the maintenance man had been made. Two hours earlier Bill Thompson, chairperson of the property committee, made the recommendation to fire him. Bob Barus, the pastor, and several members of the council were hesitant.

"Maybe we should give him one more chance," said Jane Dillon.

"Perhaps if I supervised him more closely his performance would improve," said Pastor Barus.

"Look, we all know he is an alcoholic and has been drinking on the job. As a result, he is totally unreliable," Bill Thompson replied.

During the two-hour discussion the council ranged over a number of issues. The mention of mowing the lawn led to a discussion of the Christmas crèche, where it should be located next year, and the problems with lighting. The topic of cleanliness of the church school rooms brought a half-hour debate about the day nursery sponsored by the church and whether it should be continued. Even the subject of bathroom maintenance evolved into a proposal for a senior citizens' program and supervision of the maintenance man's work moved into a session on Pastor Barus's responsibilities. At that point, Pastor Barus became defensive and suggested that the setting was inappropriate for an evaluation of his work. And so it went for most of the evening.

The procedure for managing a conflict is fairly straightforward: identify the issue, explore alternatives that will allow all parties to achieve what they want, choose an alternative, and follow it. The council meeting at Birch Road Baptist Church, however, is an example of how hard it is to put an apparently simple procedure into practice. What is so difficult? What blocks or prevents persons and groups from clarifying the issue and choosing an alternative?

In order to deal with conflict quickly, some people become "solutionizers," *pushing an action alternative before the real issue is identified.* Bill Thompson stated the issue incorrectly in the beginning—to fire or not to fire. The real issue was how to provide good maintenance at the church. His proposal was an alternative that diverted the group from clarifying the main issue. It also illustrates how moving to alternatives too precipitously can even create additional conflict.

Pastor Barus and Jane Dillon were resisting Bill Thompson's suggestion by posing alternatives of their own, but they too were not being clear about the issue. They, in effect, raised an important but still secondary issue—caring for the maintenance man.

A better procedure would have been to identify the primary concern (good maintenance of church property), lay out possible alternatives for achieving it, and choose one. If that one happened to be "fire and hire," then the group could have moved on to the issue of caring for the maintenance man. Even if the alternative chosen was to retain him, the issue next taken up could have been how to care and assist him with his problem.

Another barrier to effective management through identifying the issue and choosing an alternative is the presence of *multiple issues*. Rarely is there one crystal-clear issue in a conflict. Even if a conflict begins with a single issue, others quickly flood in. Why? Because the people are dynamic living organisms with many issues pressing in their lives. These other concerns, appropriate or not, work their way into the agenda. In the council meeting other issues as wide-ranging as the Christmas crèche, nursery school, senior citizens, and Pastor Barus's performance crept into the meeting. All may have been legitimate issues but, because they were inappropriate at that time and inadequately handled, they diverted the council's attention redundant from the primary item on the agenda.

Effective conflict management requires that an individual or group first *clarify the primary issue* and stick with it until an alternative is decided upon. As with Bill Thompson, an alternative in the guise of an issue may be presented first before the issue is clear. Keep testing the issue and alternatives by asking, "What is the issue for which this is an alternative?" or "Is this statement the real issue?"

If the conflict presents great difficulty or is very threatening, then more people will divert from dealing with it. Side issues will be raised, quick solutions proposed, or other avoidance tactics used. In such cases, continue returning to and restating the issue. "Is this the issue of primary concern and do we want to deal with it now?" As other issues are raised, acknowledge them, identify them as issues, but then ask, "Do we want to deal with them now, later, or return to the primary issue?"

In the church council no one was managing the process very effectively. Consequently, the council spent much unproductive time avoiding the main issue and chasing other concerns that should have been dealt with at another time. When that happens, people become frustrated, angry, and when possible, withdraw. Facing a conflict issue, especially one with a great deal at stake, is difficult but in the long run not nearly as frustrating and debilitating for a group or individual as unproductive wandering and not facing the issue.

6. DEVELOP ALTERNATIVES FOR GOAL ACHIEVEMENT

Search for alternatives that will allow all parties to achieve that which is important and fulfilling to them.

"Bishop, that won't work in this church." "We attempted a similar program at least twice before and it didn't work either time." "The people in the church will never go for that." "Bishop, you must recognize that this is a different church; most things just won't work here." "The people of this church are not motivated to work on its problems." These and other statements from the evening's meeting kept ringing in Bishop Harrison's head as he drove home. Even the last thing Pastor Johnson shared as he said goodbye to the bishop was, "I have tried most of those programs with my previous parishes with little response. Church people are just not as dedicated as they used to be."

Bishop Harrison had been asked by the Bloomington Church to meet with its leadership to see if he could make some helpful suggestions on how to move the congregation out of its malaise; the membership and financial-giving patterns were static. Bishop Harrison felt exhausted after the evening. He tried everything he knew, encouraging them to analyze their problems and explore new options, till finally he began suggesting program possibilities out of his long experience. Each one received the same polite but firmly pessimistic response: "Won't work; we've tried that." Stopping for a cup of coffee, the bishop finally managed a smile as he thought to himself, "One more example of the church planning style—'there is only one alternative and it won't work.'"

At the core of the Christian faith rests a confidence and trust in the future, even where there appears to be no visible hope, because ultimate hope lies not in human hands but in God's. This hope, founded on faith in God's grace, releases our creative energy to explore and risk new alternatives. It also frees us from the need to control and restrict the goals of others when they threaten our hopes. This faith believes that in the realm of God's renewing grace there is space for the fulfillment of every person.

Belief that alternatives can be discovered in which all parties can achieve what is important to them is crucial to creative management. There are numerous planning methods that can spur the creativity of individuals and groups,[6] but none of these work unless the people have a sense of hope, unless they believe that new possibilities can be discovered. The church needs first to remember and proclaim its Good News, that in God all things are possible. That sense of hope can empower the church and its members for a more creative future.

The social sciences have developed helpful tools that can be used by those who have a sense of hope and creativity about the future, one of which is brainstorming. Once the issue has been identified, brainstorming can be used to generate all of the alternatives that can be imagined or invented. The idea is to articulate as many alternatives as possible without stopping to evaluate any of those alternatives. This process encourages persons to use their creativity in sparking off each other's ideas and developing new and innovative options. The most important thing to remember is not to criticize any proposed options. Value each one. Only at the selection phase are the different alternatives measured against each other.

Practicing the skill of brainstorming is helpful in learning to manage conflict more creatively. In a conflict situation we rarely have the time or the occasion for an extended brainstorming session, but knowing the techniques does encourage persons in conflict to explore a wider number of alternatives before they rule out the unrealistic and unworkable ones.

The Bloomington Church exemplifies the attitude toward alternatives held by many churches and individuals responding to conflict. Believing "it won't work" ultimately ensures that they will experience conflict negatively. Withdrawal and apathy follow. Creative conflict management requires belief that new things are possible, as well as the skills and methods for generating alternatives.

7. INSTITUTIONALIZE CONFLICT MANAGEMENT PROCESSES

To be effective, conflict management processes must be institutionalized and not created solely for special occasions.

Rensis and Jane Lickert in their book on conflict state this proposition very directly:

> Every conflict other than those internal to a particular individual, involves an interaction among persons, groups, organizations, or larger entities and occurs within a social system.
>
> The extent to which a conflict is likely to be resolved constructively depends directly upon the effectiveness of the social system used during the conflict.[7]

The term *institutionalized* is a way of talking about building into an organization or a social system those processes, procedures, and structures that facilitate the management of conflict when it does arise. Many persons and organizations, because they want to avoid conflict in the first place, try to deny its presence until it becomes too intense to ignore. They then discover that they have no capacity, no framework for managing it.

The earlier illustration of the priest and the sister who made radically different assumptions about each other is a vivid case in point. The priest tried desperately to avoid conflict. The sister was increasingly frustrated because there was no way to confront or deal with their differences. Once the roots of the conflict were uncovered, staff members recognized their need to institute regular channels through which they could check out their assumptions and lay out their differences with each other. As a result, they designated the first fifteen minutes of every staff meeting as a time when they could share their feelings and concerns, check their assumptions, and express their hopes. It took three or four "dumping sessions" before the staff began to feel comfortable with the new procedure, and it took even more sessions before their negative feelings began to clear away and some productive work together began. The whole staff got weary of the process and kept wondering how long it had to go on. The priest never became comfortable in confronting differences, and the sister continued to feel that they did not face enough conflict. But they did gradually build a capacity to deal with those conflicts that were blocking them from being an effective team. Had they not institutionalized a way of dealing with the disagreements that inevitably arise within a group, they would have continued to destroy each other and the ministry of that parish.

In recent years *institutionalize* has sometimes been used negatively or pejoratively. I want to assist in reclaiming its positive character and to suggest that every person and organization, if they are to develop a capacity to manage conflict, must build in—however simple or complex—certain processes and procedures that will not only facilitate but force them to face the inevitable conflicts. Most persons and organizations need an "early warning system," a system in which an alarm can remind them that a particular conflict situation has the potential of being serious and destructive. Unfortunately, organizations usually leave an early warning system up to the individual and his or her good intentions. Given the fact that most individuals will avoid conflict if possible, this type of early warning system repeatedly fails. The most effective system does not count on the individual's good intentions. It must be more realistic; it must provide a means for surfacing and managing differences that will not allow individuals or the organization to avoid conflict. It can be as elementary as providing a "fifteen-minute, assumption-check-out time" or a regular evaluation at the end of each meeting. The essential rule of thumb is to provide a method and a means that *forces* you to deal with conflict and does not allow you to depend on your good intentions.

A LITURGY FOR CONFLICT MANAGEMENT

The analysis of conflict and the methods for managing it proposed in this book may appear to be completely rational, conscious, and controllable. Conflict and its management is not always rational, however. The irrational, unconscious, uncontrollable dimension of human nature shapes us far more than the rational. The aim of persons, however, is an awareness of themselves and their environment that allows them to understand, intend, and act in ways that make sense and give meaning to their lives. Conflict can destroy this well-being. How to deal with the irrational, unconscious, uncontrollable dimension in ourselves and others, to make it work for us, not against, as that becomes one of the issues of managing conflict.

Anna Marie Mason was very hesitant the first time she asked for an appointment to see Pastor Neal. Three sessions of talking about the weather, the church school, and other diversionary topics went by before she could speak of the deep distress in her life. Anna Marie loved her husband, William, very much but increasingly his sexual advances traumatized her. His physical touch felt good, but deeply wrong. William tried to be patient and understanding, but he began to feel that it must be his fault. "Am I doing something wrong? Do you not love me anymore?" he would ask.

His actions actually had little to do with Anna Marie's feelings. He was in those moments a reflective mirror onto which she projected her little-understood and inexpressible images. The returning reflections were not messages of his sending, but the mirror of her own projections. Her interpretation of his intention to love her, hold her, express his feelings, was distorted and blocked by her inward-turned eyes and ears. His saying what he wanted frightened her and turned her more inward in order to protect herself. Her wants she could hardly understand herself, much less speak of in coherent, understandable form.

Anna Marie and William rarely had angry or harsh words with each other. They took great care with the details of life for the sake of each other's comfort. But their physical separation, the invisible curtain between them, increased their anxiety and threatened their well-being and their marriage.

Management and rationality are words with little apparent application to the Masons' dilemma. They each felt alone and isolated in their problems, little realizing that they were involved in the oldest drama of humankind. They were touching and experiencing the mystery of humanity. This mysterious depth contains the energy and life-giving spirit of personhood, whose richness and potentiality cannot be exhausted by the human will. But this energy and spirit can be frequently blocked, distorted, or misdirected. Full humanity and wholeness emerge as the blocks are removed or transformed so the energy flows freely in accord with a renewed will of the person. The transformed person also opens to receive the energy and the needs of others.

Anne Marie and William are blocked and the gulf between them widens daily. In their anguish they speak for all humanity when they cry out for help, "Release me, O God, from a conflict so deep I do not even understand the issues."

A community of faith, from whatever religious tradition, evolves liturgies that enable its members to celebrate the joys and be sustained through the tragedies of life. In the Christian tradition the liturgy for worship leads us through the story and experience of human becoming and God's extraordinary response.

Thanksgiving	We are aware that all of life and the world is a gift of God.
Confession	We are other than we should be. Our efforts and energies are self-serving and destructive to ourselves and others.
Absolution	We are accepted and loved in spite of who we are. We are created for wholeness, not alienation and destruction.
Intercession	Forgiven and transformed we intercede on behalf of the needs and conditions of others.
Service	We are called beyond ourselves into the world for the sake of others.

The story of human life is the story of human conflict, both destructive and creative, both overwhelming and manageable. We need the skills of management and more—we need that which can sustain us, support us, carry us through those times when life is irrational and uncontrollable. Conflict management at its depth should be liturgical.

Liturgy has a repetitive quality that makes it so familiar and routine that it becomes integral to who we are. Then it frees us to be open to the wonder, surprises, and gifts of others, and to the depth of insight and creativity within ourselves.

A liturgy for conflict management reminds us again and again of those things that bestow creativity rather than bondage, growth rather than destructiveness. The elements of this liturgy intentionally parallel a Christian liturgy for worship.

Thanksgiving	I am an intentional person created by God with goals and a purpose. I live in a world with other intentional persons created by God.
Confession	I seek the fulfillment of my goals, even at the cost of the well-being of others and myself.
Absolution	God affirms and loves me in spite of the destructiveness of my will and actions.
Intercession	Because I experience affirmation and transformation, I am open to and care for the needs and goals of others.
Service	I will invest my creative energy in the midst of conflict to search for alternatives that lead to the fulfillment and wholeness of all persons.

For a liturgy to affect us we need to participate in it frequently and regularly. We must prepare for it, rehearse it, and use it until its message permeates our spirit and is stamped indelibly upon our actions. Also, like worship, the form and setting of the liturgy can vary greatly according to the needs and interests of the participants. A liturgy for conflict management, however we use it, should remind us of the drama of human conflict and that which makes it healthy and creative rather than destructive.

NOTES

1. H. Rhea Gray, "Basic Skills for Creative Conflict Management," an unpublished paper written for a program of the W. Clement and Jessie V. Stone Foundation, Chicago, Ill. 1970.
2. William Strunk, Jr., and E. B. White, *The Elements of Style* (New York: Macmillan, 1979), p. 66.
3. H. Rhea Gray, "Basic Ingredients of Voluntary Behavioral Change," an unpublished paper written for a program of the W. Clement and Jessie V. Stone Foundation, Chicago, Ill. 1970.
4. Carl Rogers, *Client Centered Therapy: Its Current Practice, Implications and Theory* (Boston: Houghton Mifflin, 1951).
5. Thomas Gordon, *Parent Effectiveness Training* (New York: Wyden Books, 1970).
6. One of the more elaborately and thoroughly worked out methods of creative planning and idea generation is "synectics," a hybrid word defined by its originators as "the holding together of diverse elements." For a fuller description of how the process works and the theory underlying it, see George M. Prince, *The Practice of Creativity* (New York: Collier, 1972).
7. Rensis and Jane Gibson Likert, *New Ways of Managing Conflict* (New York: McGraw-Hill, 1976), p. 15.

CHAPTER 4

Styles of Conflict Management

Individuals vary in their responses to conflict but there is a remarkable consistency to the responses of a given individual in conflict. Identifiable patterns of personal behavior tend to be repeated in certain conflict situations. These are known as styles of conflict management. Jay Hall, in his instrument designed to measure how persons act in conflict, talks about styles as "those typical and preferred ways of behaving in conflict situations which are both identified and explained in terms of the learned values that individuals apply."[1] As these definitions imply, we can identify certain conflict management styles in ourselves and other people. These patterns develop over the period of a person's life through trial and error and through modeling after other persons. Each style is an attempt by an individual to develop a satisfactory manner in which to deal with the conflict encountered in life. Behind each of these patterns lies a set of faith assumptions and values that determine which pattern will emerge as dominant.

ASSUMPTIONS, VALUES, AND STYLES OF CONFLICT MANAGEMENT

Our faith assumptions or beliefs about what is right, appropriate, and fulfilling, are key determiners of our choices about goals and behaviors. Psychological research has shown a strong need in human beings for consistency between beliefs and behaviors, so that when beliefs and behaviors differ a person will alter beliefs to parallel behaviors or change behaviors to be constant with his or her belief system.[2] Carl Rogers points out that one sign of health in a fully functioning person is a high degree of congruence between one's internal feelings and beliefs and one's external behavior.[3]

It is no surprise then to recognize that what people believe influences their approach to conflict management. As Alan Filley in his book on conflict management points out, when the two parties believe in the availability of a mutually acceptable solution, believe that cooperation is better than competition, believe that differences of opinion are helpful, believe that the other party can compete but chooses to cooperate, believe that everyone is of equal value, believe in the views of others as legitimate statements of their position, then the possibilities of creative problem solving are greatly enhanced.[4] On the other hand, if the parties believe that neither has resources that can contribute to the managing of the conflict or that neither has a commitment to use its resources, then they are likely to avoid or withdraw from conflict rather than face it.

THE CASE OF HELEN GREER

Helen Greer thought she'd tried everything. She resolved not to be intimidated by the principal. She rehearsed in her mind the responses she would make to her faculty colleagues whenever they engaged in a discussion over lunch. She pinched herself for not saying no to a request to serve on a committee at the church. "Why," she thought, "am I such a pushover?" Helen knew that despite her best resolve, she responded the same way in most conflicts. She gave in or fled.

Her response had its roots in some fundamental assumptions. Certainly she never stopped to think about them before she acted, she just acted. What determined her responses? Helen unconsciously assumed a few things. A conflict situation was not a setting in which she could accomplish anything of significance for herself. She could never stand up to the principal and say what she thought. In a debate with another teacher the right words never came. Consequently, she let them have their way and looked for what she thought were nonconflictual settings to push her points.

Deep down Helen also felt that conflict damaged relationships. If she contributed to the conflict or pushed her point too hard, she feared it might jeopardize the relationship with the principal or with her colleagues. The best policy seemed to be withdrawal, letting the storm blow over, thus preserving the relationship. Her dreams even confirmed her belief in this strategy. She often dreamed of becoming angry and talking back to her principal, who then promptly fired her.

The case of Helen Greer points to the two variables and our value choices about them that finally determine how we will act in conflict. First, for conflict to occur two or more parties must pursue their goals and compete for the same space or resources at the same time. In terms of the model suggested earlier, they are trying to occupy the box at the same time.

The other factor is the relationship between the parties. Without a setting of interdependency, however tenuous or short-termed, there is no conflict. Helen Greer, for example, may want a rowdy student expelled from her class, while the principal insists that she keep the student in class. Both things are important to Helen, her relationship with the principal and getting the student out of her class. Which does she value most? Does she have to choose between them or can she have both?

FIVE STYLES OF MANAGING CONFLICT

Jay Hall has developed a very helpful instrument, the *Conflict Management Survey*,[5] for indicating how a person is likely to act in a conflict situation. The genius of his model is that it focuses on the two key variables—each party's *goals* and the *relationship* between the two parties—that are necessarily present in every conflict. It also recognizes that the intensity of concern for the two factors varies from person to person and from situation to situation. The style one adopts is determined by the strength of concern for each of the two factors in a given conflict situation. Using again the paradigm of competing to get in the box, we can say that the styles of conflict management are the behavioral patterns we employ to occupy the box. The two determining factors are: (1) how important to us it is to get in the box; and, (2) how concerned we are to maintain the relationship with the other party who is also trying to claim the box.

The five styles[6] of conflict management follow.

The *win/lose* style is characterized by a very high concern for achieving personal goals in a conflict even at the risk of damaging or destroying the relationship with the other party. "Win at all cost; the relationship be damned," is the byword of this style. As Hall puts it, "The result is an aggressive, dogmatic, inflexible, and unreasonable approach to conflict management, in which the goal is to overcome one's adversary. The effect of such tactics on the relationship is usually not even considered until after the conflict is resolved."[7]

The *accommodation* style is characterized by high concern for preserving the relationship in the conflict even at the price of giving up the accomplishment of one's own personal goals. The relationship is of utmost importance. The person who has a strong accommodating style assumes that the relationship with the other party cannot tolerate serious conflict and, therefore, will give up pressing for his or her goals in order to reduce the threat the conflict poses to the relationship. He or she assumes that human relationships are so fragile that they cannot endure the trauma of working through differences. Often persons with this style have a high need for affiliation and acceptance and are willing to give up the achievement of their goals in order to maintain those relationships in which affiliation and acceptance are gained. Thus, the more important the relationship is to them, the more likely they will accommodate.

The *avoidance* style is characteristic of those who are most pessimistic about conflict. They feel that it is not possible to accomplish their goals in a conflict situation and that conflict is usually destructive to a relationship. Therefore, their basic strategy is to withdraw, avoid, or get away from conflict whenever possible. Often persons who adopt this style will leave a conflict psychologically even when they cannot do it physically.

Recognizing that one cannot get everything one wants and desiring to preserve the relationship, a person with a *compromise* style has the philosophy "give a little, get a little." Former President Lyndon Johnson, who characterized and practiced politics as the art of compromise, provides an excellent example. His style was always to win something of what he wanted but never press his point hard enough to jeopardize a political relationship that might be productive in the future. Compromise works in conflict but often leaves an unsatisfied taste in the mouth. It is not fully satisfying but *better than nothing.*

The *win/win* style combines a high concern for the accomplishment of one's personal goals with a high concern to preserve and enhance the relationship, which means taking the goals of the other party as seriously as one's own. It assumes that there is an alternative in which both parties can achieve their goals and it works towards that end. It assumes that facing and working through differences has the possibility of leading to a more creative solution than can be achieved by either party alone. It has a high tolerance for differences and works to promote a climate of trust and openness in which both parties can share their goals and hopes and work together for their achievement.

IS ONE STYLE BEST?

Hall's theory maintains that every person uses all of these styles and that each style is appropriate depending on the circumstances, the issue, and the intentions of the person. However, each person has an order of preference for which style he or she will use first in a conflict situation. If that style does not prove satisfactory, the person will shift to the next preferred style and so on through all the styles. For example, Helen Greer tries to balance her desire to remove a rowdy student from her class and the need to please her principal. Since her predominant style is accommodation, she will go along with the principal and keep the student. If the student continues to create havoc, she may shift to her backup style of avoidance by ignoring the student or isolating him in the class. If the harassment continues she might be sick and not come to school regularly.

Though each of the styles is appropriate under certain circumstances, research[8] has shown that some of the styles used on a regular basis will more likely promote healthy and constructive use of conflict than do others. As Helen Greer demonstrates, for example, a consistent avoidance of a persistent conflict can become destructive to the person and to the setting. This same research also indicates a rank ordering of the styles in terms of effectiveness in dealing creatively and constructively with conflict. To be most effective one would begin with a win/win style and move down the list to compromise, accommodation, win/lose, and finally avoidance, in that order.

THE IMPACT OF A STYLE

A style is sometimes experienced like the measles. We don't know where we got it, we're not even sure we have it, but the telltale signs are there and won't go away. The measles do finally disappear, sometimes leaving sad side effects. A style, though capable of being changed, hangs on, persisting despite our rational resolve. It too has side effects.

The most consistent side effect of a style is the reaction it elicits from others. A person's style tends to evoke certain styles in others. A persistent win/lose approach, for example, rarely encourages others to play win/win. Most likely, if the other parties have strong commitments to their goals, they will fight back, responding with their own win/lose action. Others will accommodate and give in. Others merely withdraw.

Even those who intend to play win/win often get hooked in the face of a win/lose style. Joe Lawrence, the associate director of the library, knew his boss very well. They had worked together for five years. They functioned amicably together in public and one-on-one. But, when the other staff were present, Joe's boss needed to put him down, to let everyone know who the real boss was. Joe would go into staff meetings determined not to get hooked. Then his boss would begin the meeting, "Joe, I noticed the number of overdue books is on the rise.

Why are you permitting that to happen?" Or, "Joe, you put the next item on the agenda. What's *your* problem?" Before he knew it, Joe would be playing win/lose with his boss. Even when Joe won the point, the boss made him feel like a loser.

A consistent avoidance or withdrawal style is like a drippy water faucet. It drives those who have to live with it to distraction. You cannot turn it off and you cannot ignore it either. It is impossible to deal creatively with differences if the other party will not join the action.

Avoidance can also be a troublesome style to read. Its author can disguise it very well in aggressive action designed to ignore the real issue and divert to another. Denial that there is a problem or projection of the blame elsewhere are also handy tools of the masters of avoidance.

An accommodating style rarely provokes hostility from the opposing party, but it is unlikely to encourage them to respond in a win/win fashion either. An accommodating style almost begs other persons to have their own way, to adopt a win/lose style.

If you want others to function in a win/win manner in conflict, win/win is the best style to employ yourself. Functioning in a win/win manner is, of course, no guarantee that others will reciprocate, but no other style is as likely to evoke a win/win response.

THE NECESSITY OF KNOWING ONE'S STYLE

We may not be satisfied with the way we react in conflict, but act we must. A prerequisite for becoming more effective managers of conflict, for changing, is being able to identify our styles, how we use them, and under what conditions.

We often use a certain style in a certain setting and a different style when the setting changes. There once was a young minister who, when working with a group of laity, was able to help them articulate their feelings and needs and to share his own. When differences arose he explored alternatives until one appeared that satisfied most of the group. When meeting with the senior minister, however, he rarely disagreed. He accommodated his senior colleague in whatever he suggested. At home, on the other hand, he wanted to be right, not to be challenged by his wife or children. There he had to win.

This is not schizophrenia, although it could become so if carried to extremes. Actually, the young minister is just being human like the rest of us who shift our styles to suit the setting. Without our being aware of the switch, however, it can have destructive potential. The young minister may only hear the support for his win/win style with laity and think that is how he functions in every setting.

In conflict our emotional involvement intensifies, our manner of acting becomes more rigid. We are less able to think, reflect on options, and choose rationally. We *act*, not think, in conflict. Consequently, it is vital to know how we are likely to act. Only then can we compensate for our inclinations. Only when the young minister becomes aware of his win/lose style at home and his fantasy of the strong husband and father that feeds it, can he alter his behavior. Only then can he feel his wife's withdrawal or understand his children's rebellion.

Unless we are aware of our styles and how we use them, our penchant for self-deception can have destructive effects. The Christian heritage has had its share of zealots for the faith whose certainty of their righteousness and others' sinfulness generated enough venom to consume both.

We even deceive our own intentions. Mary Avery, an ordained minister for almost a dozen years, continually pulled a double deception on herself. Her intention was to function effectively with others, to help them as well as herself to win. Despite good intentions, the sad thing was that Mary with regularity ended up the loser. She explained it to her friends as discrimination against female clergy. To cope with this she became more aggressive over the years. On occasion she consciously tried to play win/lose. Even then she lost.

A case in point was the time Mary was appointed to a committee to evaluate the work of the executive of their conference. The committee members quickly agreed that they needed to interview several people to gather information on the executive's performance. They could not, however, agree on whether the whole committee should interview each person or divide the chore. They finally resorted to a vote. The result was seven to two in favor of dividing into subcommittees for the purpose of interviews. Mary and Doug Hammon were the minority votes.

Immediately after the vote Mary announced she would resign from the committee if they followed that procedure.

"I don't intend to be excluded from vital information. I have been railroaded before and won't stand for it now," she said.

Her statement threw the committee into confusion. A long discussion ensued, which in the end reversed the decision. Mary won, but she lost. The atmosphere of the committee became polluted with mistrust and resentment. Members hurried through their tasks and finally left, most dissatisfied. Mary wrote the experience off as another example of ineffective church committees.

UNDERSTANDING ONE'S STYLE

Understanding our styles, how we use them, and under what conditions precedes changing our styles. A primary source for this information is obviously ourselves. We have private knowledge of our intentions and actions and their meaning to us that no one else could ever fathom. Our problem is discerning the patterns, making sense out of our actions. One method that helps is an orderly reflection on one's history. Remembering one's history in chronological sequence—the types of conflicts engaged in, the different styles used—allows certain patterns to emerge. It reveals dominant styles we used in given periods and how our styles changed. A historical look often illuminates a contemporary situation.

Self-knowledge, however, is never enough, as Robert Burns reminds us in his poem "To A Louse. "Oh, would some power the giver give us, to see ourselves as others see us." Burns's poetic insight points to our capacity for self-deception and to the fact that we can never know how our actions affect others unless they tell us. We need a loving critique from others in which they share with us how they perceive our actions and how these actions affect them.

An instrument such as Telemetrics' *Conflict Management Survey* supplies an additional source of data. Even more important, it provides a conceptual framework within which to organize the data about one's styles. The pitfall of such an instrument is that we might take it literally, assuming it furnishes the "scientific" facts about us. Any instrument, after all, is based on a theory that has its own biases.

We need all three sources, balanced against each other.

Understanding our conflict management styles takes effort, a willingness to risk, to ask for feedback, to be open to it. Yet knowing our styles is a prerequisite to altering them in order to become a more effective manager of conflict.

CHANGE: A RHYTHM OF RISK

"Can I change my conflict management style?" The question arises again and again. The answer is, "It is difficult but possible." Since styles are patterns of behavior that have become ingrained and are habitual, we resist changing them. The more comfortable they are, the more they work for us, the less willing we are to change. When we experience dissonance between what we want to happen and what actually is occurring, when we encounter negative response from others, when our pain level escalates, we begin searching for new patterns.

For those who want to change, or feel pressed to change, this section outlines the six stages of a change process. The stages are an adaptation from the phases of a learning process proposed by Billy Sharp in his book, *Learning: The Rhythm of Risk*.[9] He points out that the greatest resistance to change stems from the risk involved. There is risk at every stage, some low level, some high level, but it can block our change at any of the stages.

THREE MINI-CASES

For purposes of illustration and analysis let me preface the six stages that follow with three brief cases. One has a contemporary setting and the other two are familiar stories out of the ministry of Jesus.

Fighting the Fat

"Anybody home?" shouted the familiar voice of Edith Kramer. Sally Dawson put down her fork and moved to greet her friend at the back door. "I thought you and John were going into the city to shop this afternoon and then have dinner, but I saw the car in the driveway," exclaimed Edith as Sally met her at the doorway.

"We were," replied Sally sadly, "until John changed his mind after his golfing group suddenly got up a game for this afternoon. You want a piece of pie? I just baked it this morning."

"Sally, aren't you on a diet? Haven't you been going to Weight Watchers?" inquired Edith. Sally Dawson had been attending Weight Watchers for the past three months and had managed to lose eight pounds. Overweight had been a chronic problem for her ever since her first child was born. She knew John did not like her to be fat. He didn't say much about it, but he would occasionally drop hints or make sarcastic remarks.

Sally was a good cook—that was one of her problems. She cooked and she ate. Only in the last year or so had she begun to recognize a pattern to her eating. Whenever she was depressed or frustrated she ate for solace; then she would feel guilty and angry at herself for gaining weight.

Early that morning, when John hung up the phone and announced that the guys had a game scheduled and were counting on him in the foursome, Sally wanted to scream, but she didn't. John, staring at the floor said, "Sally, I can't let the guys down. Why don't we go out for dinner after I get back this afternoon?"

Sally couldn't actually remember what she said. She murmured something like, "That's all right, I guess," and hurried out of the bedroom to the kitchen.

As the two women sat eating pie, Sally, with tears in her eyes, looked at her friend and said, "Edith, I just don't seem to be able to fight the fat!"

The Rich Man (Luke 18:18-27, RSV)

And a ruler asked him, "Good Teacher, what shall I do to inherit eternal life?" And Jesus said to him, "Why do you call me good? No one is good but God alone. You know the commandments: 'Do not commit adultery. Do not kill. Do not steal. Do not bear false witness. Honor your father and mother.' " And he said, "All these I have observed from my youth." And when Jesus heard it, he said to him, "One thing you still lack. Sell all that you have and distribute to the poor, and you will have treasure in heaven; and come, follow me." But when he heard this he became sad, for he was very rich. Jesus looking at him said, "How hard it is for those who have riches to enter the kingdom of God! For it is easier for a camel to go through the eye of a needle than for a rich man to enter the kingdom of God." Those who heard it said, "Then who can be saved?" But he said, "What is impossible with men is possible with God."

Zacchaeus (Luke 19:1-10, RSV)

He entered Jericho and was passing through. And there was a man named Zacchaeus; he was a chief tax collector, and rich. And he sought to see who Jesus was, but could not, on account of the crowd, because he was small of stature. So he ran on ahead and climbed up into a sycamore tree to see him, for he was to pass that way. And when Jesus came to the place, he looked up and said to him, "Zacchaeus, make haste and come down; for I must stay at your house today." So he made haste and came down, and received him joyfully. And when they saw it they all murmured, "He has gone in to be the guest of a man who is a sinner." And Zacchaeus stood and said to the Lord, "Behold, Lord, the half of my goods I give to the poor; and if I have defrauded any one of anything, I restore it fourfold." And Jesus said to him, "Today salvation has come to this house, since he also is a son of Abraham. For the Son of man came to seek and to save the lost."

STAGES OF A CHANGE PROCESS

1. Assessment (Where Am I Now?)

Knowing where I am now, understanding it, making sense out of it requires me to be in touch not only with myself but my environment and my interaction with it. Generally the risk is reasonably low at this stage. I am asking myself, "How do I like the way things are?" "Am I satisfied with how I am functioning?"

Some years ago Kurt Lewin, in writing about the process of change, called this the "unfreezing" stage.[10] The very high level of discomfort is the key factor. Most of us are somewhat dissatisfied with the way we manage conflict, but until the level of discomfort becomes severe or we become dysfunctional, we are less likely to be open to change.

A second factor that creates the conditions for change is a climate of psychological safety or affirmation that supports our exploring new options. Either factor alone—discomfort or encouragement—if present in sufficient amount, can set the stage for change. Otherwise we continue to hold rigidly to old styles, inadequate though they may be, rather than risk the unknown.

From the stories of Zacchaeus and the Rich Man we are uncertain as to their assessment of themselves. There is a hint that both may be slightly uneasy with their lifestyles. They are casting about to see who this Jesus is and whether he has anything to say that might benefit them. Sally Dawson, on the other hand, is deeply troubled. Her weight problem constantly lowers her self-image. Her anger at her husband festers and gnaws at her. Giving up and getting fat continually beckons to her as an option.

These three have one thing in common. They face a potential change in lifestyle, but are unsure what troubles them in the present. They are uneasy but not sure what to do. We are all like that at times. We are dissatisfied, but not sure how to label that dissatisfaction. Moving to the next stage often helps bring clarity to the first stage.

2. Value Assertion (What Do I Want?)

We act out of our beliefs about what is right and valuable for ourselves and others. Clarity and certainty do not always characterize our actions, but we do the best we can. We strive for consistency and congruence between our values and our behaviors.

Saying what we want, or think we want, exposes us. Our actions are a clue to others, but they can never be certain of the intentions behind the actions unless we risk going public. And it is a risk. In fact, the level of risk escalates dramatically in this stage of a change process. when we have to say what we want, what our goals are, we declare what is important to us and reveal a significant part of who we are.

One of the characteristics of Jesus' ministry was to provide a setting in which persons could reveal who they were, what they wanted, and what their concerns were. The Rich Man declared directly what he wanted. On other occasions, such as with Blind Bartimaeus (Luke 18:35–43), Jesus asked people directly what they wanted.

One risk of revealing what we want is that others may reject it, laugh at us, or even resist us. If, on the other hand, they applaud us, support and affirm us, then the pressure is on to act on our declared hopes. Either way we risk failure or ridicule. No wonder it feels safer to guard our intentions, not to risk change.

The story of Zacchaeus tells us little of what might be on his mind. On the surface he appears to have a limited goal of just seeing this Jesus about whom he obviously had heard. Zacchaeus' life is typical of many of our lives. We are not quite sure of the deeper motive behind our surface interest or concern, but taking the risk to share that desire can uncover the more profound need. Sally Dawson's immediate concern, for example, was always losing weight. Her conversion of calories to fat appears as the source of most of her life's grief. She does not perceive her conflict management style as a significant issue, certainly not one she would try to change. Until Sally identifies that as a problem, gains some insight about her current management style, and desires to change it, she will continue accommodating and avoid encountering her husband. In turn, the calorie intake will remain high as compensation.

3. Concepts, Theories, Understanding (How Do I Get There?)

When we plan to drive to some distant, unfamiliar place, we most likely rely on a roadmap to guide us to our chosen location. A roadmap is one way to use the knowledge collected and arranged by others to assist us in arriving at our chosen destination. Without it we would spend a great deal of time and energy through trial and error searching out our own direction. A roadmap provides a conceptual framework that charts the landscape and shows the relationships among elements of that landscape. Our language serves a similar though more comprehensive purpose of charting, arranging, and relating our experience and knowledge of reality.

This stage of the change process necessarily relies on the knowledge and wisdom of others. It provides information related to where we want to go and what we want to achieve. The collective wisdom not only provides a conceptual roadmap and the location of various points of interest, but also theories about their relationships and the best means for proceeding from point A to point B.

Sally Dawson can easily become stuck at stage one or two unless she looks at a roadmap with new glasses. Her friend Edith Kramer could be a resource by proposing a theory. "Sally, in your case eating is avoiding. Your problem is John, not weight." This sudden insight sends Sally in a new direction. "How can I change my style of managing conflict with my husband? Losing weight is a side trip—important, yes, but now secondary."

For the Rich Man and Zacchaeus, Jesus is perceived as the source of wisdom. He knows something they do not know which might help them. The Rich Man doesn't mince any words or waste any time. He pops his burning question straight away, "What do I have to do to gain eternal life?" Zacchaeus is less clear about what he wants. The story says he just wants to see what Jesus looks like or who he is, but he gets more than he bargained for. Rather than leaving him a spectator, Jesus makes him the focus of attention. Jesus provides new input. "Zacchaeus, you are somebody. You are important as a person. I care about you and I want to spend some time with you." This changes Zacchaeus' perceptions completely. His life and future look new; he can see himself clearly as he is. Then he asserts what he wants to be and declares his intent to act on it.

Jesus looks deeply into the Rich Man and responds, "You

can't get there from here. You have been working hard but still hedging your bets. Getting where you want to go requires a totally different vehicle. The theory for you is "giving away is the way to get."

This third stage of change can be full of surprises. Its risk level, however, is lower than the previous stage because it doesn't require great personal investment. We are merely looking over the landscape, searching for resources, ideas, theories, and new options that can help us figure how to where we want to go. The risk rises dramatically in the next stage when we have to put those theories into action.

4. Personal Experiencing (What Actions Must I Take?)

This stage requires that theory be put into practice. Enough studying of the map and hypothesizing about which route is best. The time has come to select a route, make a choice, begin the journey. The risk level escalates dramatically. Even when countless others before us have traveled this route and left explicit instructions for us to follow, this time we are the travelers. Perhaps we will get lost. We might have an accident. Others may make fun of us. Nothing is more threatening than trying new behaviors for the first time.

Once Sally Dawson grasps the fact that her style of managing conflict with her husband, and not losing weight, is the real issue, she has to decide whether to take action on it or not. Her change effort requires that she take new action, that is, not accommodating or withdrawing from her husband. Such action can and should be simple at the beginning. For example, to test the theory and practice a new style she might commit herself to remain in the room for five minutes with her husband once a conflict begins, rather than withdraw hastily to the kitchen. This initial step does not change her complete style immediately, but it does initiate a new behavioral pattern which, if successful, could lead to a style change.

Zacchaeus and the Rich Man move in opposite directions at this stage. The Rich Man rejects the behavioral consequences of Jesus' theory. The price is too great; he will not pay it. Zacchaeus, on the other hand, declares he will change his style and will back it up with an immediate behavioral change. "I will give away half my possessions and repay anyone I have defrauded fourfold," he says.

The risk of putting theory into practice is worth it, if it works. The next two stages are concerned with whether it works or not.

5. External Evaluation (How Do Others Respond to My Action?)

A new behavioral pattern that is rejected or responded to negatively by significant others is difficult for us to maintain. Perhaps the most powerful deterrent to change for the Rich Man is his image of what his friends and relatives will say and do if he starts giving away all his possessions. Imagine the uproar in a middle-class American home to Dad's announcement; "No camp this summer, no new prom dress, no vacation, no new furniture. We are selling the house, buying a less expensive one, and giving the difference to the inner-city poor."

Regarding the story of Zacchaeus, Frederick Buechner suggests, "It is not reported how Zacchaeus got out of the sycamore, but the chances are good that he fell out in pure astonishment."[11] In the process he fell into the arms of a loving and sustaining community. Only such a community would affirm and support his new behavior though, as Luke implies, not all were straightaway so eager to affirm.

Most new behaviors we try out are not so radical or life-changing as those of Zacchaeus and the Rich Man, but the same principle applies. New behaviors, if they are to become new patterns, need the affirmation and support of significant others. Otherwise our internal resolve to act in a new way melts in the face of steady opposition from those who matter most to us.

Sally Dawson's new behavior of remaining in the room with her husband for five minutes during a conflict, rather than fleeing, most likely surprises him. "What is Sally doing?" he thinks to himself. "She is acting differently. What is it supposed to mean?" Meanwhile, Sally is watching his reaction like a cornered animal deciding whether to fight, run, or be friendly. The signal from her husband that is most important to Sally is what this new behavior will do to their relationship. If it does not appear to threaten it very much, Sally may continue to hang in. If it appears to have serious adverse effects, she will probably withdraw again.

Another factor, however, seriously influences her behavior and counterbalances any response her husband may make. How did the new behavior feel to her?

6. Reflective Recycling (Did It Satisfy Me?)

The cycle of change ends where it began, assessing where we are in relationship to our environment. Reflecting on whether an action satisfies us or not is an assessment of our new status. Do we want to repeat the behavior? Does it help us be and do what we want?

If we feel deeply enough about a new direction, if it embodies our faith assumptions, we can sustain it even in the face of a negative response from those significant others. The chance of a new behavior becoming a new pattern, of course, is greatly enhanced when it has both internal and external affirmation. Sometimes one source of support is enough, though not usually.

The stories of our three characters stop at this stage. We do not know their futures. We have no idea whether the Rich Man, having rejected the risk of a new direction, is able to rationalize his old pattern and be content in it. My hunch is that he does not change his status but he becomes more deeply troubled about it. Once aware of a deep level of dissatisfaction in our lives, we find it hard to cover up, deny, or rationalize it away.

Zacchaeus, on the other hand, has the potential of dual confirmation from himself and the new community. We are not told if Zacchaeus becomes a faithful member of "the way." But he gives the theory a really good test—"giving away is receiving." If I were placing bets, I would put them all on a new lifestyle for Zacchaeus.

Sally takes a mini-step toward a new style. If it works, she may take another and another, slide back one, and take another. The satisfying taste of a new way of interacting may whet her appetite for more. Without a doubt such actions will require some adjustments in her husband's style of interaction. Change in a person is rarely confined to the individual. Its reverberations flow outward in all directions like the ripples from a stone tossed in a pond.

CHANGING STYLES: A SUMMARY

Like most of conflict management, understanding the concepts and principles is easy—it's the doing that's difficult. The better part of wisdom for changing a conflict management style is to remember the process, keep it simple and focused, and work at it steadily—not in bursts of enthusiasm. If you desire to change, try to follow these steps:

1. Identify your current conflict management styles and how you use them in different settings. Are you satisfied with them?
2. Identify which style it is you want to change and to what.
3. Identify what behaviors would be characteristic of the new style. What actions would enable you to do and be who you want to be?
4. Practice these behaviors first in settings that have lower risk and are supportive.
5. Practice these behaviors in daily settings. Develop means of getting feedback on the impact of your actions.
6. Are you satisfied with the results? If so, reinforce or support these new behaviors so that they become natural patterns of action.

NOTES

1. Jay Hall, *How to Interpret Your Scores from the Conflict Management Survey* (1969), p. 1, copyrighted by and available from Teleometrics Inc., P. O. Drawer 1850, Conroe, Tex. 77301. It comes as part of a set with the *Conflict Management Survey* produced by Teleometrics, Inc.

2. Alan C. Filley, *Interpersonal Conflict Resolution* (Glenview, Ill.: Scott, Foresman, 1975), p. 6.

3. Carl Rogers, *On Becoming a Person* (Boston: Houghton Mifflin, 1961), pp. 339–342.

4. Filley, op. cit., pp. 60–70.

5. Jay Hall, *Conflict Management Survey* (1969) copyrighted by and available from Teleometrics, Inc., P. O. Drawer 1850, Conroe, Tex. 77301.

6. For a more extensive description of each style see Hall, *How to Interpret Your Scores from the Conflict Management Survey*, pp. 2–4.

7. Ibid., p. 2.

8. Ibid., p. 4.

9. Billy B. Sharp with Ward Weldon, *Learning: The Rhythm of Risk* (Rosemont, Ill.: Combined Motivation Education Systems, 1971).

10. Kurt Lewin, "Group Decision and Social Change" in E. E. Maccoby, T. M. Newcomb, and E. L. Hartley, eds., *Readings in Social Psychology* (New York: Holt, Rinehart and Winston, 1958), pp. 197–211.

11. Frederick Buechner, *Wishful Thinking: A Theological ABC* (New York: Harper & Row, 1973), p. 99.

Part II

Theory in Practice

Introduction to Use of Cases

This book sets forth some theory, but its goal is effective practice. Reading about, even understanding theory, does not make someone an effective practitioner of an art. The culmination comes in the life experiences of those who appropriate theory and finally incorporate it in activity. Thus, the book does not stop with presenting and illustrating theory. It aims to move readers a step closer to its final application in life experience. Cases as "slices of life" in which to practice theory are offered to "try out" better ways of coping with conflict. Understanding and practicing the applications in these cases can be an intermediate step from theory to practice in life.

ADVANTAGE OF CASES

Cases have the advantage of being compelling, provocative dramas of human life that we can enter into and use to test our theory without running the risk of confronting the issues in real-life settings. Rehearsing a performance before the audience arrives gives us a feel for the role and accustoms us to the moves and action until they can be risked under the pressure of a real presentation.

Good cases, though they are about other people, places, and

settings, have a way of drawing us in. Without noticing the transition, we begin to think of a case as our case. We identify with the characters. We experience their feelings, grapple with their issues, and make decisions much as if they were our own. The norms, places, and times of the conflicts differ, but many of the issues are similar to those we ourselves encounter in the world.

The cases presented in the book were prepared by trained case writers.[1] Designed as the basis for discussion rather than to illustrate effective or ineffective handling of a situation, they have no simple or single solutions. Rather, as is the case in our own lives, the cases require decisions, choices, and commitments to an answer and an action. The conflicts present in the cases can, of course, be avoided—they are not our problems, it doesn't affect our lives if they are worked out or not. But they or conflicts like them will reappear at some points in our lives. The cases merely provide a protective setting in which to consider the issues, explore several alternatives, and then risk a choice without paying the ultimate consequences in real life. Learning requires risking. Use of the case merely reduces the level of risk in order to encourage people to practice.

Cases used in a group setting can provide a mirror in which to reflect on ideas, feelings, and actions as the participants encounter and differ with the ideas and actions of others. The group also provides new perceptions, options, and possible actions that an individual alone cannot generate.

TYPES OF CASES

The theory of conflict management set forth in this book is intended to apply broadly to all levels of human life, from individuals to social structures. The target for its use, however, is the life of the church. The selecting and ordering of the cases are thus designed to address areas of concern and ministry for the church. They raise questions and issues with which pastors and laity as individuals, and congregations as corporate bodies, must deal if they are to be the church and perform its ministry.

Each case has conflict within it. The cases are diverse, providing various types of conflict, varying issues, and multiple settings, while focusing on different areas of ministry. The cases are intended to be normal rather than exceptional or exotic. The conflict issues are often subtle rather than overt. In short, these cases, all of which were actual events though somewhat disguised here, are intended to provide the users with settings, analogous to their own life experiences, in which to practice.

Conflicts within the church often become intense, threatening, even destructive, not because church people are more conflict-prone but for the simple reason that the church's ministry deals with the significant issues of life. They are issues of ultimate importance to us. Even though the church tends to repress or avoid conflict, the very depth of the issues forces it into the open, often in jagged, unrecognizable, or even destructive forms. As a result, pastors, laity, and congregations need sensitivity and openness to conflict and the commitment and skills to deal constructively with it.

The cases selected for this book deal with ministry. They obviously cannot cover the full range of ministry issues, though, so the selection focuses on some of the crucial areas in the church's ministry. Chapter 5, Foundations for Ministry, contains two cases that deal with the issues of belief and Christian community. The case *For the Life of the Church* is about a church officer who is concerned about the pastor's theology of resurrection. The pastor is effective in other areas of ministry and the officer wonders how important doctrinal issues and beliefs are. Should she push the issue and risk a serious conflict in the church?

In the case *To Move or Not to Move?* a family, a parish, and a whole community are confronted with the threat of dramatic change which, in turn, forces them to grapple with the meaning of Christian community and loving one's neighbor. Black families are moving into a previously all white neighborhood. Many white families panic, sell their homes, and move.

Chapter 6, Ministry to the Church, presents cases dealing with the internal life of parishes in the areas of caring, education, and youth. The case *New Life Treatment Center* has its setting in a Christian agency, not a parish, but it, nevertheless, raises in a subtle but probing way the issue of caring for persons. As an alcoholic treatment center the agency deals with that concern directly, but more importantly the case indirectly raises the question of how institutions care for those employees who carry out their mission. In short, how are the carers cared for?

In *Let's Close the Sunday School!* the pastor's unilaterial decision to close the Sunday school leads to strong parent protest and raises the thorny issues of the nature and purpose of the church and how children are nurtured and educated in the faith.

The case *Lock-in* raises the difficult issues of youth ministry—program design, teenage values, discipline, the role of parents, and frustration of the leaders.

Chapter 7, Ministry to the World, contains two cases that explore the mission of the church, its nature, and focus. *Operation Reach-Out* portrays a parish struggling to clarify and commit itself to a mission. A conflict boils around the meaning of evangelism and how that congregation should engage in evangelism. Is it merely to gain new members, which they need, or what is its purpose?

No Room at the Inn depicts a church caught in a dilemma. On the one hand it claims a commitment to the world but discovers many of its members backing away from a ministry to run-away youths in their neighborhood.

Chapter 8, Management of Ministry, has three cases that contain conflict issues arising out of management concerns in the church. *Do We Need a New Pastor?* deals with the role of pastoral leadership in a congregation, conflicts between senior and assistant pastors, and who manages such conflicts in a parish.

When the Congregational Meeting Erupted is a case about a congregation concerned about keeping itself alive and vital. They decide that an extensive goal identification and planning process is what they need. They develop a thorough and well thought out planning scheme. They do everything right, but things still fall apart in the end.

For the Love of Money pictures a church that, through the help of a stewardship consultant, increases its budget dramatically. The same consultant, however, leads the pastor and several members into some questionable personal investments.

USE OF CASES

Cases are flexible learning instruments; they can be used in many different ways and in multiple settings. The cases in this book lend themselves well to a group setting where there can be discussion and interaction. The diverse resources of a group—different perceptions, ideas, feelings, assumptions, expectations, and hopes—increase the value of the lesson learned from the case. A teacher or leader of a group can select a case for a particular purpose and design the group's use of the case around that purpose. Some formats for group use follow.

General group discussion can be designed to identify the conflict issues and how one might manage them. In such an approach the teacher's role is not answer-giver but prober, catalyst, and facilitator, stimulating the group to use its creativity to analyze the case.

The group can be divided into *subgroups* and each given a specific task such as "identifying the issues" or "developing alternatives." Or, a combination of total group and subgroups can be used, with the total group responsible for identifying issues and the subgroups working on alternative resolutions for the specific issues, or any combination of these tasks.

Another approach is to look at it from the *viewpoint of each character* in the case and list the issues and alternatives as that character might see them. Such an approach can remind the participants that even issue identification and alternative development are done from one's own unique perspective. This process itself usually generates conflict among the participants about interpretations.

The group can *role play* the case, which gives individuals an opportunity to practice their conflict management skills and receive feedback from the group. In using role playing the leaders should:

1. Secure the agreement of the group members to use role playing. They may be reluctant at first and need encouragement. Do not force or manipulate persons into role playing.
2. Make sure all participants have read the case and grasp the essential information about the characters, settings, and issues. The issues may be left unclarified if the role play is designed to identify and work with the issues.
3. Secure the agreement of group members to play the various characters in the case. Having them volunteer is best. More encouragement and support may be needed.
4. Define the task for the role play group. Are they to work on an already defined problem? Are they to identify a problem? What's their goal?
5. Terminate the role play at an appropriate time. Each participant should be given an opportunity to "debrief" his or her experience in order to move out of the role as well as to hear others' reflections.
6. The group can then use the experience of the role play to move in several directions—further analysis of the case, reflections on personal learnings, or reflection on theory and general learnings.

A group can use a case for discussion purposes without having a designated teacher or leader. However, the clearer the members are about their purpose for using the case, the more likely it is that it will be a good learning experience. The leader-led group has an advantage. The leader can guide the process and thus release group members to enter freely into the discussion.

Individuals can also use the cases by themselves with great benefit. Since the cases are true-life situations, individuals working alone to improve their conflict management skills can use the cases as an interim step between understanding the theory and putting it into practice in their own lives. The following framework is suggested as an approach for those who use the cases for learning how to manage conflict more creatively. The framework is designed for use by individuals, groups with or without a leader, or teachers designing a learning experience for others. It is intended to be flexible and adaptable—my hope is that users will not feel compelled to employ the framework rigidly or legalistically. It and the cases should be used according to the needs and goals of the users. The framework is based on the theory of conflict and its management developed in the first part of the book and its aim is to aid persons to become artists of conflict management.

FRAMEWORK FOR CASE ANALYSIS

1. Identification of Conflict Issues

Managing conflict requires that we be able to identify the primary issue or issues in the situation. An issue is that point where the goals of two or more parties try to occupy the same space, compete for the same resources, at the same time. One way to identify issues in a case is to look at the characters and ask what their goals are. What are they trying to accomplish? Where do their intentions and actions intersect and thus create the conflict? In some cases a conflict issue is intrapersonal, that is, internal in a person. Two or more conflicting hopes, fears, or wants compete within the same person. In other cases the conflict is interpersonal, between two or more persons, between two groups, or between a person and an organization.

Sometimes with cases groups have a tendency to keep dissecting the situation, continuing to identify issues without zeroing in on a central issue. A leader should push a group to choose the issue that seems most important and to pursue management strategies for that situation. Working with a case can thus provide an excellent opportunity to practice sticking to one issue and working it through rather than jumping to peripheral issues. The case experience can thus help prepare for many of the conflicts in real life, where we avoid facing the main issue by working at lesser ones.

2. Development of Alternatives

Developing alternatives means finding a way in which all parties can achieve most of what is important to them. Role

playing is an excellent way for the participants to practice identifying what a person wants and how it feels in conflict when
this is blocked. Reflecting on an experience in a role forces us
to be in touch with our intentions and how we try to achieve
them even when acting as another person.

Developing alternatives also uncovers the styles we use to
manage a conflict. It is often helpful at this stage to introduce
or remind participants of the different styles we use in managing conflict. Ask them to reflect on which styles the characters
in the case or they themselves are using when trying to develop
an alternative to a conflict issue.

3. Principles of Conflict Management

We become more effective managers of conflict to the degree
that we can inculcate the principles within our actions. The
cases should be used as an occasion to remind and review the
principles for the participants. The method can vary. Perhaps
one principle can be taken at a time and explored to see how it
could be used in the case and what effect its usage might have
in that conflict. The participants may also practice one or more
principles in subgroups or in a role play around the issues of
the case.

Like rules of grammar, the principles are used continually
but need to be reviewed again and again until their correct use
becomes habitual. A summary of the principles is included in
this part of the book immediately preceding the cases. One may
find it helpful to post them, make a copy for each individual, or
continually refer the user to them in the book as one works
with the cases.

4. Styles of Conflict Management

A summary of the styles of conflict management, as discussed earlier in this book, is also included in this section. An
outline of styles will remind participants that they all have different styles of managing conflict and that they will use one or
two styles more than the others. They need also to remember
that becoming a more effective manager of conflict requires an
understanding of the various styles and how, when, and under
what circumstances we use them.

A case is a good chance to practice style identification. For example, examine each character in the case and determine which style or styles he or she appears to be using. Speculate on differences it might make in the case if he or she employed alternative styles.

Analyzing the characters in the case is a first step but then the participants must move on to exploring their own styles. This can be done by reflecting on what style they might use if they were a particular person in the case. One can also use a combination of methods, perhaps giving the participants an instrument such as the *Conflict Management Survey,* or having them write their own conflict history (see Chapter 4 for details). Then have them use their increased knowledge about themselves to explore how they would handle a case using their predominant style and how they would manage it if they used another style they would like to develop.

5. Resources of Faith

Our faith assumptions and perspective ultimately determine what is important to us. Faith structures our meaning systems and determines our actions. The resources of our history and tradition, our religious experience, and our contemporary symbols and expressions of our faith story are the reservoir from which we draw our assumptions and nourish our perspective. Considering a case as a "slice of life" is an occasion to probe how the resources of faith manifest themselves in that setting and how the persons in the case use or do not use them. It is also an occasion for the participants to explore their own faith assumptions and perspectives and how these affect the way they would respond and act in such a setting.

Whether one reads the case privately or with a teacher guiding a group through a case discussion, the question of one's perspective of faith is central to the management of conflict. Christianity is an incarnational faith. It looks for the continuing manifestations of the Spirit in the flesh and blood of life. Whether "doing a case" or acting in life, the Christian tries to be open to that Spirit which illumines one's perspective on life, gives visions and goals toward which one strives, and sustains one's action in the midst of the inevitable conflicts of life.

Delve deeply into the resources of faith in the case and in your own life.

6. Contract for Action

It is tempting to read cases as interesting illustrations, to think about them as detective stories, or discuss them in an analytical and academic manner. When we fall prey to these temptations and stop at that point, a case has little impact on how we manage conflict. Changing the way we manage conflict has cognitive, reflective, and analytical dimensions, of course, but it must finally evidence itself in action. Thus, in using cases to learn to manage conflict more effectively, the design should include an action phase. An action phase can grow out of and build on case analysis. With these goals in mind an individual reader or a discussion leader might try the following procedure:

Enter the case as fully as possible. Allow yourself to identify with persons or positions as you feel moved to do so. Try to remove as many restraints in yourself as possible. Be who you would be in the case.

At various stages in the discussion of the case, perhaps after a role play, or at the conclusion, *ask what you have discovered about yourself* in the following ways:

1. What conflicts of my own did I get in touch with? How might I apply the principles and draw on my faith in relationship to them?
2. How do I act in conflict? What style or styles do I tend to use? Is this the way I want to function?

If areas of desired change are identified, *describe specifically what perspective or behavior you want to change.* Then *develop an action plan,* perhaps reinforced with support and accountability from others, *to practice this new perspective or behavior* in order to change your style. Or, plan to practice one of the principles in relationship to a specific conflict. (It even helps to discipline yourself to put these plans in writing.)

One final admonition. *Begin in simple fashion.* Focus on one task—a principle, a new behavior as evidence of a new style or a new assumption which you will test.

A CONCLUDING SUGGESTION

The most productive learning occurs when the readers enter each case as openly as possible in order to test their insight, risk their analyses, practice their conflict management skills and then, alone or with others, reflect on what they have learned from the experience. The purpose of cases is to simulate real-life experiences of conflict. Encountering a case is like confronting the countless conflict situations in our own lives. In life we have to make our own judgments and commitment to our own action. The intent is that the cases will be a setting in which practice and reflection in a lower risk environment can increase our insights and skills for other life experiences.

A brief note is added after each case, although it is not intended to do the work of analysis and reflection for the reader. Its purpose is to move the reader into the ministry theme and how that theme applies to the case and its conflicts. A set of suggestive questions are included, not as an exhaustive list, but as a stimulus to the reader to ask his or her own questions about the case and seek his or her own answers.

Finally, have fun with the cases. Use them for learning and growing. After all, they may become your own cases.

NOTES

1. All the authors of the cases in this book have been trained at the Case Study Institute and its successor, the Case Method Institute. In 1971 the Sealantic Fund gave a grant to the Association of Theological Schools to establish the Institute for the purpose of training teachers in theological seminaries in the case study method. Since 1978 the Case Method Institute has included pastors and lay persons in the training as well. Cases written by the Fellows of the Institute are presently listed in annotated bibliographies published by the Intercollegiate Case Clearing House, Boston, Mass. 02163.

Summary of Principles for Conflict Management

THEORETICAL ASSUMPTIONS

Persons are intentional, goal-directed beings. They will seek to do and accomplish that which is important and fulfilling to themselves.

Conflict is two objects trying to occupy the same space at the same time. Conflict is inevitable in human life, but people *can* learn to deal with it creatively and constructively rather than destructively.

PRINCIPLES

1. HELP OTHERS FEEL BETTER ABOUT THEMSELVES.
   Persons and organizations manage conflict best when they are feeling good about themselves.
2. STRIVE FOR EFFECTIVE COMMUNICATION.
   Effective communication consists of in-depth and reflective listening and sending with the knowledge that one's perceptions and messages are uniquely one's own.
3. EXAMINE AND FILTER ASSUMPTIONS.
   Unexamined assumptions contribute to destructive conflict.
4. IDENTIFY GOALS, WHAT IS WANTED.
   Identifying what a person, group, or organization is trying to accomplish, what is wanted, in a situation is an essential element in conflict management.
5. IDENTIFY THE PRIMARY ISSUE.
   Until the primary issue has been identified and acknowledged by the principal parties in the conflict, it is difficult to manage the conflict.
6. DEVELOP ALTERNATIVES FOR GOAL ACHIEVEMENT.
   Search for alternatives that will allow all parties to achieve that which is important and fulfilling to them.
7. INSTITUTIONALIZE CONFLICT MANAGEMENT PROCESSES.

To be effective, conflict management processes must be institutionalized and not created solely for special occasions.

Summary of Styles of Conflict Management

THEORETICAL ASSUMPTIONS

Every person, group, or organization copes with and manages conflict. That management takes the form of a variety and combination of styles.

All styles are appropriate depending on the context and issues. Every person uses all the styles to some degree, but will tend to have a dominant style, using the others to varying degrees as backup styles.

The typology of styles is built around the recognition of two factors present in every conflict: (1) the goals each party is trying to achieve in the situation; and (2) the relationship the conflicting parties have with each other.

The style adopted is determined by the relative concern a party has for these two factors in that particular conflict.

STYLES

Win/Lose. Characterized by a high concern to achieve personal goals and a low concern for the relationship. "Win at all cost; the relationship be damned" is the byword of the style.

Accommodation. Characterized by a high concern for the relationship and a willingness to give up personal goals for the sake of the relationship. Fearful that the conflict might damage the relationship.

Avoidance. Characterized by a hopelessness about conflict. Assumes we cannot accomplish personal goals or preserve the relationship in a conflict. Best policy is to withdraw and avoid if possible.

Compromise. Assumes we cannot get everything we want in a conflict. Better to "give a little, get a little." Push for some of your goals but do not push so hard as to jeopardize the relationship. Allow the other party to get some of what they want.

Win/Win. Combines high concern for the accomplishment of our goals with high concern to enhance the relationship. Assumes both parties can achieve their goals in the situation and works toward that end.

CHAPTER 5

Foundations for Ministry

There are varieties of gifts, but the same Spirit. There are varieties of service, but the same Lord. There are many forms of work, but all of them, in all men, are the same God. In each of us the Spirit is manifested in one particular way, for some useful purpose.

For Christ is like a single body with its many limbs and organs, which, many as they are, together make up one body. For indeed we were all brought into one body by baptism, in the one Spirit, whether we are Jews or Greeks, whether slaves or free men, and that one Holy Spirit was poured out for all of us to drink.

1 COR. 12:4–7, 12–14

For the Life of the Church (Belief)

ALICE FRAZER EVANS

Anne Sommers's hands trembled as she slowly closed her notebook and prepared to leave the Charlottesville Methodist Church administrative board meeting. She thought to herself that her strong reaction to events of the monthly meeting must be a combination of concern, anger, and frustration. What was the pastor's view of the resurrection? Was the personnel committee trying to bury a "hot potato"?

Background

Anne's thoughts flashed to the precipitating phone call she had received five weeks earlier from Fred James, a young law-

ALICE FRAZER EVANS is an Adjunct Faculty member of The Hartford Seminary Foundation, Hartford, Connecticut. Case copyright © 1978 by the Case Study Institute.

yer in the congregation who was in Anne's parish group. He'd said that she was the one church officer he knew well and he'd like her to present his letter of resignation from the church at the next board meeting. Aware that she had not seen Fred in church for several weeks, Anne invited him to meet her in town for lunch and talk about his decision.

During lunch the following day Fred shared that he was unable to worship in a Christian congregation led by a man who was not a Christian. His conclusion was based on statements made during a Bible study class led by Pastor Alan Williams and several subsequent conversations he and Williams had. Anne pressed Fred for more specific information and Fred reminded her that four months after the new pastor had come to their church he announced an introductory Bible study seminar for adults. Williams opened the first session by passing out a questionnaire "to get some idea what people think about various Christian terms."

Fred James recounted that he had suggested to Pastor Williams that it was only fair for him to complete a questionnaire as well. When the group began to share responses, Fred pushed the pastor specifically to answer one of the questions, "Who do you think Jesus Christ was?" Alan Williams responded, "I believe that Jesus was who the early church community said he was. He was a human being like us but one through whom something special had happened. We don't know all the details about his life and work, but we do know they had terrific impact on a community of people."

Fred then told Anne that when he asked the pastor if he believed Jesus was physically raised from the dead as scripture told us, the answer was, "No, if you mean that literally; yes, if you mean it symbolically."

Art McFadden, also a member of the seminar, then angrily called out, "You can't be any kind of a Christian if you don't believe in the resurrection." Fred noted that several members of the group commented on Art's response; others seemed either uncomfortable or perplexed.

Fred recounted that he had later met with the pastor in his study and that Williams had also come to his home to visit. At these meetings Fred told the pastor that he believed the Bible literally and that he had experienced the Holy Spirit directly in his life. Fred also shared that he was spiritually enriched from attending pentecostal and charismatic worship services. The pastor had listened to Fred, but Fred felt that Williams did not show much sympathy for his position.

Fred told Anne that he felt he could not continue worshipping under Williams's leadership. He knew that Art McFadden was already going to another church. Fred said he had considered calling a meeting of several church friends whom he thought would be supportive of his position. However, he decided that gathering forces would be divisive, unconstructive, and possibly not successful. During the following three weeks Fred told Anne he read scripture and prayed about the issue. Fred then decided the most responsible move would be to resign with a letter to the board indicating his reasons.

In his letter Fred cited Pastor Williams's denial of the "actual resurrection of our Lord" and wrote that Williams "was vague and theoretical in his understanding and pronouncement of the gospel." Fred declared that a clear, strong affirmation of faith was crucial for those called to lead a Christian flock. In reference to his attitude about the church, Fred had concluded his letter by quoting Revelation 3:16: "Because you are lukewarm, and neither hot nor cold, I will spew you out of my mouth."

Whose Responsibility?

As Fred handed the letter to Anne he said, "I want you to know that I don't blame Alan Williams personally. He has been open and honest with me about his faith. I blame the church. In your pastoral search you did not deal seriously with doctrinal issues. The church board will be failing again in its responsibility if it does not face the pastor on this issue. You cannot ignore something so central to the life of the church. As a body of elected lay leaders charged with the care of our congregation, I can't believe the board will do nothing." Deeply disturbed with Fred's comments, Anne assured him that board members would receive his letter.

Anne remembered the following week as one of struggle. She particularly recalled her conversation with Ted Andrews, a layman who was secretary of the board and a close personal friend. Anne shared with Ted her anxiety about the issues Fred had raised. Anne said that she clearly didn't believe every word in the Bible literally, but "there are some things central to my faith and one of them is my firm conviction in Christ's resurrection." She affirmed, "It's because of this resurrection that he is now alive for me in the presence of others and he ministers to me through them." Anne wondered if in their search for an efficient administrator, a decent preacher, and someone with a strong ego, the pastoral search committee had failed to make Williams's statement of faith an issue. "Ted, have we gotten our priorities mixed up?" she asked. "We're not an organization that needs an administrator, but a community that needs a committed Christian."

Anne asked Ted if he thought the board should deal openly with the issue as Fred James demanded. Or should it come to the whole congregation for them to consider? What was the best process for dealing with this important issue?

Ted responded, "I don't agree with you about the pastoral search committee and their work. I know they discussed Alan's statement of faith at length with him; they may not have touched specifically on the resurrection, but they did talk about his theology. It also seems to me that Alan has tried to be honest with Fred about his faith. Do you think Fred could have misunderstood what Alan said? Maybe Fred heard what he wanted to hear. Anne, maybe you should talk directly to Alan; I don't think you'll feel right about it until you do."

"I can also see why we shouldn't dredge up the whole issue before the congregation. Look at our situation. We're a struggling, inner-city church, barely holding our own financially, with 160 deeply committed and very strong-minded members. I think it took a great deal of courage for Alan to accept the challenge of a call to this kind of church from an associate pastor's position in a comfortable suburban church. We are at last beginning to recover from Pastor Edward's resignation two years ago. Alan is just establishing his identity with the congregation and is still extremely vulnerable. Maybe you're blowing this issue up out of proportion to its importance to the life of the church and its future."

Evaluation of the Pastor

Ted reminded Anne that the personnel committee of the board would soon begin its regularly scheduled pastoral evaluation. "Why not give Fred's letter to Ron Howard, chairman of the committee," Ted suggested. Anne agreed.

That evening Anne called Pastor Williams and made an appointment to see him the following morning. In recalling Fred's comment about the Bible study class, Anne considered the possibility that the new pastor could easily have been taken off guard by Fred's antagonistic style of "legal grilling." Anne also thought about Art McFadden who was one of the most fundamentalistic members of their congregation. A mechanic in a local garage, Art based his "born again conversion" on his brother's miraculous healing from leukemia which doctors had declared as incurable. When Art had been received into membership two years ago he had made a somewhat unusual request to affirm his faith by a personal testimony before the congregation. At that time he declared that "God is alive in the scriptures as he dictated them. We are saved only through belief in the risen Christ." Though Anne felt that she respected both Fred and Art's beliefs, she knew that a literal understanding of scripture was inconsistent with her own theology and that of most other members of this mainline urban Protestant congregation.

With this in mind, Anne called two other members whose judgment she valued. She asked about the first session of the Bible study group. They both confirmed Fred's version of the pastor's comments.

When Anne met with the pastor the following morning, she told him of Fred's letter. He indicated he was sorry to hear of Fred's decision to resign, but thought it might be for the best. There was always attrition when a new pastor came. Williams added that the Bible study class had begun two months ago. At the time he had considered the incident insignificant and quite frankly had forgotten exactly what he said. However Williams did acknowledge that he could well have said that he did not believe in the literal interpretation of the resurrection. Williams said that further discussion might be helpful, possibly through another personal conversation or even a seminar in the church some Sunday morning. Pastor Williams and Anne then spent the next hour discussing the upcoming stewardship campaign.

The pastoral evaluation involved interviews with all church officers as well as an interview with the pastor. The process took three weeks. Prior to the final report of the personnel committee to the board, Anne stopped Ron Howard after Sunday worship one morning, asked him to step into the vacant church office, and inquired about the review process and the letter from Fred James. "Anne, we discussed this in our meeting last week," he said. "The pastor shared his views with us, we had conversation back and forth about it, and none of us thought his view was too extreme for us. I must admit I get a bit lost in the theological discussion, but Williams made sense to me. I plan to report to the board that we had the conversation, but I don't plan to get into any of the details. If someone wants to press the issue he or she can, but I don't think it will serve anyone's cause. I'm pleased with Williams's work. I've seen some good things happen, one of which is the addition of twelve new members in the first six months of his ministry. Frankly, I'm satisfied with his leadership."

The following Wednesday evening, during the course of the personnel committee's favorable report to the board, Fred James's letter was read aloud. There was discussion during which the pastor stated that under the church's constitution there were two alternatives regarding James's request for resignation: receive the letter of resignation, accept it, and inform James; or appoint a delegation from the board to have further discussion with James to see if he would not reconsider and to investigate the matter further. The Board unanimously chose the former. As one member on the board put it, "Fred has already had conversation with Anne about this. I don't think further talk with any of us would shed any further light."

The board voted to accept the report by acclamation, but

following the vote, several board members asked to return to the issue of the letter. Anne Sommers remained silent. Ten of the fifteen board members had not been aware of the letter prior to this meeting and several pressed Alan Williams for clarification. Lisa Warren, who headed the Christian education committee, spoke out. "I would agree that we do not want to raise this as a major issue with the congregation, but Alan, I would like to hear what you do believe about the resurrection of Jesus. Can you give us a statement?"

Alan Williams responded firmly, "No, I really couldn't give an adequate one in a few minutes. The personnel committee and I have dealt with this at some length. They have submitted their report which you have all voted to accept. I am planning a sermon on the topic of the resurrection in the next few weeks. You can hear my views then. We have an extremely heavy agenda tonight. We should now move to the next item of business."

The next hour and a half was a blur in Anne's mind. The meeting flowed with the usual speed and efficiency of Pastor Williams's style. Anne's thoughts were filled with a jumble of the doubts of the past five weeks. "How important are theological issues? As a faithful Christian with my own theological understanding, how widely can I differ in my understanding from my pastor? Alan Williams has been honest about his faith, and I do see why he wouldn't want to open a hornet's nest at this point in his ministry. But have we dealt adequately with this issue? Am I abdicating my responsibility as a church leader by not pressing it further?"

The board meeting was closed with prayer. Most of the members had already gotten their hats and coats. Ted Andrews, secretary, with notebook in hand, had been questioning each officer. He turned to Anne. "Are there any particular items you want to docket for our next meeting?"

EXPLORING THE CASE

Belief is not just assent to a set of doctrinal statements, but at its deepest level is an expression of our faith perspective on ourselves, our world, and the divine. It shapes how we perceive ourselves and our world, what we value, and the actions to which we commit ourselves. Our faith is grounded in a historical tradition and is expressed within that framework. The way it is expressed, the very choice of words and the emphases we give them, even how we say them publicly, are all sources of potential conflict, often the most intense conflict.

Some of the conflict in the Charlottesville Methodist Church emerges from deeper-level theological and philosophical issues. For example, what is the source of truth for individuals and the church? How do we know it?

As you explore the case, how would you define the issue between Fred James and Pastor Williams? Is it a conflict of personalities, or are there basic differences in their faith assumptions? How do other members of the church get pulled into and expand the conflict? What other issues are spawned?

Every institution has to balance its needs for unity and diversity. It must have enough agreement and commonality among its members in such areas as goals, norms for behavior, and faith assumptions to hold it together. Yet it needs diversity for creativity and growth, and diversity causes conflict. Examine how the Charlottesville church is coping with this dilemma. What conflicts does it raise?

Explore this case for these deeper-level issues and the ways they might be addressed in that congregation. In trying to manage this and similar conflicts you might ask:

1. Which persons in the case have the best chance to pose alternatives that can resolve the conflict?
2. What conflict management principle would you advise a person such as Pastor Williams to employ?
3. Which persons are using the most destructive conflict management styles?
4. What resources of faith are available to help in the conflict?
5. What would you do if you were a member of that church board? What does your projected action reveal about the way you manage conflict?
6. Identify one area in your own theology that creates con-

flict for you and others. Contract to explore it more deeply within yourself and with others.

Possible Uses of the Case

- In an adult education setting to stimulate discussion of theological issues and the conflicts they raise.
- As a training tool for church councils or other key leadership groups exploring the questions of authority, governance, pastoral selection, and evaluation.
- For individuals to explore their own beliefs. As an individual try outlining some of your key beliefs and where they
  are in conflict within yourself or with the beliefs of other
  persons or institutions. Then try to apply the conflict management principles to these conflicts.

To Move or Not to Move? (Christian Community)

G. DOUGLASS LEWIS

Bill Riley slowly hung up the telephone and turned to his
wife. "That was Carl Pleamons. They decided to sell their
house and move." For three years the Glendale community in
which the Rileys lived had been undergoing dramatic change.
Black families were moving in as white families left for the
suburbs. Bill and Margaret Riley, as the representatives from
St. Timothy's parish to the Glendale Ecumenical Council, had
urged neighbors who were white not to sell their homes or
move. Now the prospect of their oldest and dearest friends,
Carl and Janet Pleamons, moving stunned the Rileys. It confronted them in a very personal way with the question of
whether they should move or stay.

Glendale Community

Glendale, a community of some thirty-five thousand people,
was actually a residential section of a large midwestern city.
For over sixty years it had been a stable community. Its major
growth had occurred at the turn of the century as immigrants,

mostly Irish and a few Germans and Scandinavians, moved to the city to work in its rapidly developing industries. Its tree-lined streets, parks, churches, schools, locally owned shops, and single family homes had supported its residents' claim that Glendale was an excellent place to raise a family.

St. Timothy's Roman Catholic Church, located in the center of Glendale, served nearly two thousand families. Its parish school continued to thrive. Noted as a liberal and progressive parish, its leadership—both clergy and laity—were active in community affairs. It became the first parish in the diocese to establish a parish council and was one of the founding members of the Glendale Ecumenical Council. Father McAuliffe, the beloved pastor at St. Timothy's, encouraged the lay leaders to be involved in parish and community affairs.

Because of the school, the stability of the population in the neighborhood, and an emphasis on Christian community in the parish, St. Timothy's had an unusual sense of closeness among its members. As Bill Riley said, "Of course, we have our differences, but basically we are like one big, happy family."

A Changing Neighborhood

Glendale had been unaffected by the dramatic changes that occurred in other parts of the city during the 1950s and 1960s. Following World War II, blacks from the South moved to the northern cities in increasing numbers. Settling first near the central city, they gradually expanded outward. Many black families, as their economic status improved, looked to the neighborhoods with single family dwellings as a step towards improving their living conditions.

In the spring of 1975 the first black family bought a house in the northern section of Glendale. By the fall of 1975 real estate agents began systematically calling home owners all over Glendale inquiring into the possibility of persons selling their homes. At first they made offers several thousand dollars above the going market price. However, as an increasing number of homes were sold to black families the price began to decline until some houses brought only half the price of the first homes sold in the community. The local newspaper and the Real Estate Board condemned the "block busting." Although several real estate agents were "warned" by the board, the practice continued. By 1977, 25 to 30 percent of the homes in Glendale had been purchased by black families. A sense of crisis and panic grew daily among the white families.

Response to the Crisis

In October 1977 the issue was placed formally on the agenda of St. Timothy's parish council. Three weeks prior to that meeting Father McAuliffe had preached a homily on the issue of integration and housing and called on the parish to deal openly with the issue as a Christian community. He again spoke at the council meeting urging the leaders present not to panic. He reminded them that all persons, black and white, male and female, Greek and Jew, slave and free, were one in Christ. Bill Riley said at the meeting, "If we all hold firm and do not sell, the community will stabilize. We can have an integrated Christian community." Others expressed doubts at the meeting that such a stable community was possible. They pointed to other areas of the city that had changed from white to black in the course of a few years. Finally the parish council decided to ask Bill and Margaret Riley, as their representatives on the Glendale Ecumenical Council, to raise and discuss the issue there.

The Rileys were able to place the issue on the ecumenical council's agenda at its December 1977 meeting. After a lengthy discussion the council voted to request each member parish to discuss the issue in a manner appropriate to the parish and to urge the parish members not to panic and move. The council asserted its belief in a stable, integrated Christian community, and that such a community was possible in Glendale.

The Rileys did not stop there. They, along with Carl and Janet Pleamons, sponsored a series of meetings in their homes to which a large number of families active in St. Timothy's were invited. The meeting became a time for candid exchanges on the issue. The Rileys and Pleamons argued that their Christian faith provided the basis on which they could build a stable, integrated community in Glendale. Both were stung most deeply by the words of Michael Williams.

"I'm not a rich man. Most of my savings are tied up in the house. If property values continue to decline, my future financial security will be wiped out. Isn't it better to salvage something while we still can?" Bill Riley knew Michael Williams articulated the feelings of many people in Glendale.

Meeting With Pastor James

In its continuing attempt to address the problem, the ecumenical council in the spring of 1978 invited the Reverend Earl James, pastor of the newly established black Baptist Church in North Glendale, to meet with the council and discuss the problem. During the discussion one council member suggested a quota system in which all churches, real estate agencies, and other civic groups would cooperate to try to restrict the number of homes sold to black families to 30 percent of the homes in the area, thus stabilizing the community. Pastor James immediately rejected the idea.

"Black people," he said, "have suffered enough and a quota system is just another form of discrimination. All our people want and deserve is decent housing. Why can't we live together as Christian people? After all, it is the white people who are causing the problem by panicking and fleeing, not black people who are merely buying homes that are for sale."

The Rileys and Pleamons said little as they drove home from the meeting together. Bill Riley confessed to Margaret as they arrived home that he was depressed.

"The problem seems overwhelming, as if a great flood is sweeping over us and we are powerless to stop it," he said.

For the next month the Rileys saw very little of the Pleamons. The Pleamons attended mass at a different time than was their custom. Carl Pleamons missed the April parish council meeting. Then came the phone call.

"Bill, I don't know how to tell you this. But Janet and I have just received a good offer on our house. We have decided to accept. Bill, it's inevitable. You and Margaret had better get out while you can."

Bill Riley was stunned, but deep down he had to admit to himself that he too had been considering for the first time the feasibility of a move. He and Margaret stood there looking at each other and wondering.

EXPLORING THE CASE

At Hartford Seminary our staff has worked with dozens of parishes assisting them in assessing themselves, identifying their priorities, and planning how to invest themselves in ministry to achieve their priorities. Again and again the top priority turns out to be the desire for a deep and sustaining community. The hunger for community is almost rampant in our culture. Yet many barriers, social and personal, block or hamper the emergence of community. Conflict is a signal that such barriers are present.

One approach to the case is to explore the barriers to community in the case. Barriers can be as diverse and subtle as different understandings of the nature of community, unconscious assumptions and prejudices, the desire for stability and fear of change, the threat to financial security, the inability or unwillingness to be vulnerable to others. As you identify some of the barriers ask how they engender conflict. Who does the conflict affect—individuals, groups, institutions, or the whole city?

In what ways are the characters in this case attempting to deal with the conflicts? In this and other conflicts around the issue of community you might ask:

1. How can the experience of conflict be used as an early warning signal that barriers to community are emerging? Search for the blocks in order to identify the primary conflict issues.
2. How can you remove the barriers and manage the conflict? What alternatives do you see in the case for managing the conflict?

3. Which principles would you recommend be used, by whom, and in what setting?
4. Are the resources of faith being used helpfully in the case? What resources are present? How ought they to be applied?
5. In working with the case, what barriers to community did you uncover in yourself, your church, or your town? How are these causing conflict?
6. Identify one of those barriers to community and commit yourself to lowering it.

Possible Uses of the Case

- In conjunction with a Bible study of Paul's great image of the body and the variety of gifts in 1 Corinthians 12.
- With a church that is struggling with the problem of unity and diversity within its life, or with a community that is undergoing change.
- With individuals and groups dealing with racism and the destructive conflicts it creates.
- For individuals to examine their own hidden barriers to Christian community.

CHAPTER 6

Ministry to the Church

They met constantly to hear the apostles teach, and to share the common life, to break bread, and to pray. A sense of awe was everywhere, and many marvels and signs were brought about through the apostles. All whose faith had drawn them together held everything in common: they would sell their property and possessions and make a general distribution as the need of each required. With one mind they kept up with their daily attendance at the temple, and, breaking bread in private houses, shared their meals with unaffected joy, as they praised God and enjoyed the favor of the whole people. And day by day the Lord added to their number those whom he was saving.

ACTS 2:42–47

New Life Treatment Center (Caring)

WILLIAM R. LENTERS

Roland Jenner, executive director of the New Life Treatment Center, Inc., a Christian agency for the chemically dependent person, was ambivalent about a management decision that he must make soon. He was worried that his decision could possibly cause emotional pain and trauma to Mary Rogers, an employee of New Life for over ten years. The problem emerged in January 1980 when the center began facing the next fiscal year. Its budget showed a deficit of over $100,000. The only alternatives open to the treatment center, it seemed, were either to cut back on services to clients by July or raise 58 percent more money in donated income by December.

WILLIAM R. LENTERS is an Associate Pastor of the Palm Lane Christian Reformed Church in Scottsdale, Arizona.

A cutback meant eliminating service to long-term clients. The possibility of transferring Mary to another department seemed plausible but, in fact, was impossible. Mary was trained to provide social services to long-term clients, but was not qualified to do conventional therapy. Since a cutback would mean the elimination of long-term care at New Life, it would also mean phasing out Mary's position. This decision was difficult and further complicated by a history of painful events in New Life's recent past.

A Changing Philosophy

Historically, New Life's management style had been "family" oriented. Decisions were made on the basis of ownership and consensus, and its fifteen-year history was marked by quality Christian service to the alcoholic. Its beginnings were tied to the treatment of the skid-row alcoholic.

Mary was initially hired as a secretary by New Life's "grand old man" and founder, Sven Johnson. Johnson was New Life's patriarch and Mary's father figure. Although Sven no longer had any official authority at New Life, he was still an important figure about whom Mary said, "Sven has done for me what my father never did; he gave me a feeling of being someone and being able to make a contribution." He helped her reach beyond her job as secretary to become a friend of the suffering alcoholic. Mary learned well the art of social services. She willingly donated overtime to the center at the expense of her family. Her husband often called the center and complained because "supper was never on the table." Mary was well received by the clients because she "cared so much." She took on more and more responsibility such as serving as a court advocate and community and referral resource person on behalf of New Life's clientele.

In 1976 Roland Jenner assumed the position of executive director. At that point New Life's direction and style changed. Roland sought to transform its image and program from a "mission approach" that focused on Bible study and moral teaching to a treatment center that used Alcoholics Anonymous and conventional psychological therapies expressed from a Christian perspective. The staff increased in size from six persons to twenty-four, half of whom were counselors. Its budget increased from $200,000 to $700,000.

Within this framework Mary's role and function were viewed by the counseling staff as less important than in previous years. In fact her style was a handicap. She appeared to foster dependent relationships with her clients. As Mary began to feel more and more isolated and even defensive about her position, she used Sven as her buffer and protector. At staff meetings he would assert, "Mary does more good around here for our residents than two counselors put together." In May 1978 Sven Johnson died. Mary felt alone. She retreated into her work and away from her colleagues. She missed staff meetings and in-service training sessions. Her comments were usually prefaced by, "No one pays attention to me anyway, but . . . "

In his effort to restructure the center's program and philosophy, Roland periodically expressed a desire to the executive staff that New Life "get rid of Mary" for what he termed her "reactionary and unprofessional relationships with the clients." He pointed to Mary's oft repeated phrase in staff conferences that "we should not discharge 'Joe' because he is so cute." In Roland's judgment she no longer fit the New Life profile. Still, he had no real grounds to terminate her because she was effective within the framework and territory she had cut out for herself. The tension between Roland Jenner and Mary Rogers grew. Mary's annual performance appraisals between 1976 and 1978 were increasingly critical. "Mary, you must work on not protecting clients by doing for them what they must learn for themselves," was Roland's summary statement.

Grievance

Roland further enforced his decision by not granting Mary a raise in salary though he did give her a cost of living increase. This action angered Mary. Not feeling safe with Roland, she went directly to the board of directors to register her grievance. She claimed she was being treated unfairly because she was a woman. Roland was angry. He confronted her and told her that going before the board directly had violated New Life's grievance procedure.

Mary responded, "Roland, I cannot talk to you. You will

only ignore my request for a higher salary and use it to find some reason to get rid of me. New Life is my life and I will fight for my job and what I know I deserve. I've worked longer than anyone here and I feel I need a raise and deserve one." Mary continued petitioning the board for the salary increase as well as a new job title that more accurately reflected her actual job. "I'm no longer a mere secretary," she asserted.

The board unanimously rejected Mary's request and deferred to Roland's recommendation not to grant her a raise. Mary did not feel that she could abide this decision. She therefore filed a sexual discrimination grievance with the Equal Employment Opportunity Commission. Roland first heard of Mary's action when the EEOC summoned him to a hearing in order to learn the facts of the case from his viewpoint. Prior to Roland's appearance before the EEOC, he contacted the center's lawyer, Steve Pogson. He informed the board that he had done so. Upon hearing and reviewing what Roland had told him about Mary's history, Pogson indicated in a written report that Roland was justified in not granting the request and that Roland was not acting in a discriminatory manner towards Mary. His brief also indicated that because of Mary's limited education (high school only) and actual job description, Mary was adequately compensated. Her salary was actually commensurate with that of professionally trained counselors on the staff. Mr. Pogson's advice was, "stand fast, hold your position; she does not have a case that she can win if she decides to litigate the matter."

Board of Directors' Reaction

By this time the board was getting anxious about the EEOC becoming involved. They reacted negatively to this advice from Pogson. The board was concerned about the constituency of New Life that supported it financially. This constituency contributed more than half of New Life's income. They were a force to be considered, reasoned the board, and they would not take kindly to the news that there was staff dissension requiring litigation in a secular court of law.

Board chairman Jerry Doyle was getting angry and tired of

the situation, especially all the complaintive calls he was receiving from Mary. "Jenner," he said, "You don't have your staff under control and I have serious questions about your ability to manage New Life." Accordingly, the board chastised Jenner and they contracted the services of an outside consultant, Mr. Steve Scott. Scott's task was to effect a reconciliation between Jenner and Rogers in order to avoid litigation in the courts. He was also instructed to assess and evaluate the management style in effect under Roland's leadership. Before Steve Scott began his task, the board voted to grant Mary Rogers a $1500 increment.

Scott utilized his time to determine the center's strengths and weaknesses. He gave special attention to Roland's style of management and its effectiveness. The results of his month-long study were documented for the board. His findings indicated that Roland was doing an adequate job of managing New Life and bringing its programs up to date with effective treatment modalities for the addicted person. Following the consultant's analysis, recommendation for a staff policy manual with a new grievance procedure and outline of employee rights, and Mary's wage increment, Mary dropped the grievance with the EEOC.

Financial Crisis

It had been two years since the grievance issue was formally resolved, and the relationship between Roland and Mary had softened and warmed. When Mary contracted cancer in the spring of 1979, Roland encouraged her with visits and an extended leave. He also provided counsel and a listening ear as she discussed her ensuing divorce from her husband.

In January 1980 a new problem emerged. It threatened to aggravate the old wound between Roland and Mary. Roland's business manager reported that the financial problems that New Life would be facing in its current fiscal year were serious. Mary had been back on the job for three months following her surgery. In response to the fiscal problem raised, Roland called an executive staff meeting to consider the alternatives available that would meet the crisis: sell the property and relo-

cate in smaller office space, raise the needed $100,000, or cut
back in services.

Since sale of the property would take at least one year
(downtown property moves slowly), and the possibility of raising the donational level 58 percent was unlikely, the only feasi-
ble alternative seemed to be a cutback in services which could
save the center $75,000. The service that was costing the center
money and could be cut back without jeopardizing New Life's
identity as a healthcare agency was the long-term care unit. It
was in this unit that Mary served.

Roland Jenner looked once more at the critical situation involving the financial crisis of the center and the personal problems of Mary Rogers. He carefully pondered his responsibility
as a Christian manager and employer of a woman with a troubled career at New Life, while at the same time weighing the
responsibility of fiscal management in an agency with cash-
flow shortages.

EXPLORING THE CASE

Caring for others lies at the core of Christian ministry. For
Christians the ministry of Jesus personifies caring. Yet the
ministry of caring causes conflict. Jesus' reaching out to certain
individuals and groups alienated and angered others. His willingness to risk caring and to interpret the ministry of caring in
a new way paved the way to the cross for him.

Most Christians would acknowledge the need for being cared
for and also their desire to care for others. The dilemma and
the inevitable conflict arises over what caring is and how it is
done. When is well intended caring actually destructive? Is caring always person to person? How do institutions and social
structures provide caring, or don't they? Who is responsible for
institutional caring?

All these questions pertain to the New Life Treatment Center. It is an agency designed for caring for a particular needy
group but, as with all institutions, it is faced with issues of
caring for those within its own organization and the conflict
that this generates. The case can be used to explore the issues

that arise around caring and conflict. In using the case you might ask:

1. What issues about caring need addressing most urgently in the case?
2. Is there sexism at New Life Treatment Center as Mary Rogers charges? If so, how is it expressed? Does it block caring and create conflict?
3. Which conflict management principles would you apply in the case and in relationship to what issues?
4. What styles of managing conflict are present in the case and which are most caring in nature?
5. From your faith perspective what is a caring ministry? How would you apply it in this case?
6. In your life, where are there individuals in conflict who need caring? Commit yourself to a ministry of caring to those individuals, either directly or structurally.

Possible Uses of the Case

- With a church or other organization to explore how it cares for its employees.
- To train laity in the ministry of caring inside and outside the church.
- For individuals to reflect on and learn about the relationship of caring and conflict; how conflict may be a mode of caring; how conflict may be a signal that caring is being blocked.

Let's Close the Sunday School (Education)

G. DOUGLASS LEWIS

Reverend Don Watson was stunned and hurt. He sat in his living room rereading the letter (Exhibit A) signed by thirty-three members of the parish criticizing his work as rector. These members were the core of young families in the parish.

He had baptized many of their children, visited them when they were sick, worked with them, and yes, even fought with them on occasion. Just one week ago he had met with them to hear their concerns. But now, this critical letter left him hurt and dismayed.

Background

Don Watson had been rector of St. John's Episcopal parish for nine years. The parish, located in an upper middle-class suburb of Providence, consisted of executive and professional people. In Don's words, "Many of our younger members are bright, capable, energetic, handsome people who are determined to make it in life. They are overextended financially and in their time commitments, but their greatest weakness is a tremendous fear of failure." In his first five years in the parish Don was driven to succeed himself. He worked tirelessly to initiate programs and see that they were successful. The parish was a hub of activity.

"I used charm and energy to make it and we had a classy program that was constantly being written up in the diocesan paper. It was a real ego trip for me. About four years ago, however, I experienced a growing sense that this was not a faithful ministry. Things have been different ever since."

The Decline and Fall of the Sunday School

No area of the parish's ministry had been a greater struggle for Don Watson than the Sunday school. Recruiting laity as teachers was a chore. They resisted giving much, if any, time to teacher training. One year after he became rector the parish hired a part-time associate minister with primary responsibility for education. According to Don, Bill Jones was a dedicated and hard worker, bent on "succeeding in the ministry." He spent an enormous amount of time each year recruiting and training lay persons as Sunday school teachers. When necessary he would meet every week with individual teachers, at their convenience, to assist them in preparing for their Sunday classes. Recruitment became so difficult that he could seldom secure a commitment from a lay person to teach more than two consecutive weeks. Again and again, the same response was given by laity: "I don't know enough about the faith to teach someone else."

The rector and his associate decided a change was in order. The educational emphasis should be on adults and their growth and maturity as Christians. Perhaps, then, they could and would educate their children in the Christian faith. An extensive adult education program was instituted.

About two and a half years after this decision Bill Jones accepted the call to be rector of another parish. Don Watson turned to a lay couple, Fred and Jane Horn, who had worked closely with Bill Jones. They agreed to direct the Sunday school with assistance from a lay woman from the community who had some previous training in Christian education. The vestry hired her for six months as a consultant. The leadership of the Sunday school had changed but the problems did not. Teachers remained difficult to recruit and attendance continued to decline.

At the end of that year Fred Horn did a study of attendance patterns in the Sunday school. He discovered that very few children attended three consecutive Sundays. He also learned that when one child in family was absent, all children in that family missed. These statistics matched the lifestyle of many of the families in Warwick. They traveled a lot. In the summer there were vacations. In the winter there were ski weekends. Don Watson concluded, "The people of St. John's parish want a Sunday school for their children when they are in town and it is convenient."

Decision Time

Fred Horn recommended that the parish decide if it wanted a Sunday school or not. The vestry set a meeting date after Sunday worship one month hence. The meeting and its purpose was publicized via a letter to the members and announcements at Sunday services. When the date arrived, about 130 persons attended worship but only 30 remained for the meeting afterwards. About 10 persons, most of whom were over sixty years of age, spoke in favor of retaining the Sunday school. After speaking, they left the meeting. The remaining 20, many of whom had young children, voted to drop the Sunday school and to use the next year to explore what option the parish might develop for an overall educational program. Ralph Meyer, a layman, wrote a summary report of the meeting and it was mailed to all members of the parish.

Within two weeks a group of parents who had not been at the decision-making meeting met with some who were at the meeting to explore how to help the children in the regular worship service. Many who came were angry at the decision and demanded an alternative worship service for the kids. The rector reluctantly agreed to an alternative service to be conducted by volunteer parents but stressed it was not to be a Sunday school.

The group worked some during the summer designing a program. When they showed the design to the rector, it appeared to him to be a pseudo–Sunday school. Nevertheless, he agreed to allow it if the staff would come to a weekly training session he would run. The group refused to give that amount of time. He then offered a one-session training course. Four of sixteen potential staff showed for the training session. Still the program was conducted in the fall. Every report Don Watson heard about the program throughout the fall increased his unease. To him it was clearly a disguised Sunday school program and not an alternative worship experience for children. The members of the congregation and even members of the alternative worship staff referred to the program as "Sunday school."

"I could not tolerate their 'God will get you if you are not good' theology any longer," he said. "I felt I was being derelict in my duty to allow that kind of teaching to go on." In January he called in the woman who was coordinating the program and announced that the program was canceled as of that moment. "At that time," he said, "I offered an alternative—have a clearly understood babysitting/entertainment center for children who can't stand church or whose parents are uncomfort-

able with their children being in church with them. They
rejected the alternative."

The Gathering Storm

The reaction was immediate. Members telephoned one another discussing the action pro and con. Small groups gathered
in homes to air their feelings. Some individuals met with the
rector to share their unhappiness. Opinions varied as to what
should be done. A majority of the vestry supported the rector's
decision. Some, like Frank Foster, wanted to hire a "professional" to run a Sunday school. Others, like Bill Stanton, thought
"some people want the church to be a full-service organization
to meet their needs and to which they have to contribute little.
The Sunday school failed because the parents were not committed to have their kids there or give time to staff it. If they
are unhappy, they should look for another parish."

The most unhappy and frustrated members centered in a
group of couples who had children of Sunday school age. They
gathered in the home of Rick and Laurie Carroll on three different occasions to air their feelings and decide what to do.
Rick summarized many of the feelings in the group.

"Many in the parish are upset with the rector. He seems to
spend more and more of his time with a selected few. Less and
less is offered for kids. Some have already left the parish and
many others will follow if something is not done soon."

Some wanted to go to the bishop but the group finally decided to invite the rector for a face-to-face meeting at the Carroll
home. They went at it for three hours. Rick reported, "Don did
not seem to hear us. We asked for a Christian education program for our children and he talked of a committed group of
families who would participate in education as a whole. We
pointed out that a group tried to develop and run a program
and he dismissed it."

The group, frustrated and angry, met again without the rector and decided to draft a letter to the rector stating their
grievances. Thirty-three signed the letter.

Don Watson was stunned and hurt by the letter. How had

his ministry come to this after giving nine of his best years to this parish? He wondered what his next move should be.

EXHIBIT A

Reverend Don Watson
St. John's Church
Warwick, Rhode Island

Dear Don:

We, the undersigned members of St. John's Church, feel with a deep sense of concern that a crisis of serious proportions has developed within our church.

The specific problems leading to this conclusion are numerous, and, we believe, are only symptomatic of an overriding problem: namely, that St. John's is failing to meet the needs of an increasing proportion of its membership. This is all too apparent when one considers the large number of active parishioners who have left and the growing numbers who are considering leaving our church to seek Christian community and spiritual fulfillment elsewhere.

Reasons supporting this concern include the following:

— Lack of a viable Christian education program for our youth and adults.
— Cancellation of selected worship services.
— Lack of rector visiting all parishioners in need.
— Increasing authoritarianism on the part of the rector.
— Lack of support by the church leadership of various programs.
— Availability of the rector to parishioners.
— Unclear role and function of both the rector and the vestry.

Our most serious concern is our conviction that the current leadership of St. John's has been unresponsive to the parish by its failure to deal with these problems in a conservative manner. We would like to point out that motivation starts at the top and works down through the ranks. Without some form of guidance, along with encouragement and support, by leadership, people become discouraged and reluctant to get involved.

We urge you to consider our pleas most seriously. We bring them to you in the prayerful hope that together we may heal the wounds of separation afflicting our church community.

We feel the need to plan ahead for the immediate future. We, therefore, express our expectation that within a month you will present a viable plan for discussion with us.

Yours in Christ,

EXPLORING THE CASE

The Sunday school often is the focus of much conflict in parishes. At least for the last hundred years or more in Protestant churches in the United States the Sunday school has consumed much of the energy of congregations. As a program area it has demanded, commanded, and mobilized much of the time and energy of laity in the ministry of the church. Furthermore, it is a highly charged emotional issue. Parents invest so much emotion in their children, and they look to the Sunday school to provide education and nurture in the faith for them. It is no wonder that intense conflict is generated around the Sunday school.

Let's Close the Sunday School shows that the Sunday school alone is rarely the issue. It may be the spark that ignites or reveals other issues. In exploring the case you might ask:

1. What do the different parties in St. John's parish want? How different are they in their goals for the church? What conflict has this led them into? Are some of the conflicts internal to the individuals, and if so, how do these fuel other larger conflicts?
2. On which issue would you focus first? What alternatives are there for managing the conflict around this issue?
3. How would you apply the conflict management principles to these conflict issues?
4. What are some of the faith assumptions underlying the wants of the persons in the case and the conflicts? Do they, for example, have different understandings of the

nature of the church? What are they assuming about how persons are nurtured in the Christian faith?

5. What styles of conflict management did the rector employ? How helpful were they? How might he have functioned differently? Would it have changed anything?

6. What do you believe about the nature and purpose of the church, and what are the implications for how persons are nurtured in the faith?

7. Are there places in your life or your church where you can commit yourself to provide, either personally or structurally, the means to nurture others in the faith?

Possible Uses of the Case

• For training members of a board of Christian education, and Sunday school teachers.

• To initiate a discussion among pastors and laity about the role of a Sunday school.

• For individuals to explore their understanding of the church and Christian education. Ask yourself about your own internal values and conflicts, and how these get expressed in the life of your congregation.

Lock-In (Youth)

WILLIAM CROMER

"Have you seen the guy wearing the red shirt?" Beverly inquired anxiously of Mary.

"No, I saw him before the movie started, but I don't see him now." Quick glances around the room revealed that Tommy was indeed missing as well as several others.

"Where could they be?" Mary asked, as they hurriedly be-

WILLIAM CROMER is Professor of Christian Education at Southern Baptist Theological Seminary, Louisville, Kentucky. Case copyright © 1977 by the Case Study Institute.

gan to search. Jack returned in a short while only to relate that they could not be found anywhere within the church building.

The Setting

Mary Cauthern, part-time minister of youth at First Baptist Church, had been making plans for a lock-in for the senior high youth for over a month. It had been scheduled to be held at the church on a Friday night after a home football game. The youth seemed anxious to come and bring friends to share in this time of all-night activities.

The pastor had been very explicit with Mary. Adult members of the church must be present to help supervise the activities and see that "nothing went wrong to cause the church any embarrassment." Also, he made it clear that a detailed-to-the-minute program was essential to the effectiveness of the lock-in. The pastor always checked Mary's outline for activities to be sure they were appropriately planned, and he was willing to help ensure a program's success through proper planning.

Mary, a seminary student, came to First Baptist as a summer youth director. The church then asked her to continue working with the youth in the fall on a part-time basis until other arrangements to hire a full-time worker could be made. This would be Mary's first lock-in, and she, too, wanted it to be an evening the youth would enjoy. She formed a flexible schedule of activities to be sure that the whole evening progressed from one activity to another to keep the youth interested and involved.

Enlisting Adult Leaders

The recruitment of adult chaperones presented a problem because many who would work well with the youth were not available for that particular Friday night. Mary was trying to avoid using parents if at all possible. Finally, three adults agreed to attend and help—Jack Hunter, part-time minister of education and father of one of the boys attending; Beverly Snyder, mother of a senior-high girl who would not be attending; and Donna Owens, a new Sunday school teacher for the senior-high girls who was anxious to get to know the girls better.

The Lock-In

The lock-in was to be held in the large lower auditorium of First Baptist Church which had the convenience of kitchen facilities, rest rooms, and, of special importance, all doors could be locked in the area. However, there was one door located off the lower auditorium that locked to outsiders but could be opened from the inside.

By midnight nearly forty youth, almost half of whom were visitors, were locked in. Mary gathered the group to establish some ground rules and to introduce the visiting youth, the adult leaders, and two other friends of Mary's who were to sing and lead in the group singing. The rules included no sleeping, and if anyone left the building through the one door possible or caused any unnecessary trouble, his or her parents would be called and the youth sent home.

The first hour of the evening seemed to progress well. Then Joyce, one of the visitors, asked Mary, if it was okay to smoke. When Mary explained that no smoking was allowed in the church building, Joy asked if they could go outside to smoke. Mary again explained the ground rules and nothing more was said.

After a time of eating and group singing, Jack interrupted the group in an out-of-breath voice, "We want this evening to be an enjoyable one, but I have found two outside doors to the church propped open with sticks. I don't know who is responsible, but we need to cooperate in observing the rules of the lock-in or else we'll all have to go home." The group seemed stunned at this but agreed that they would cooperate in keeping such an incident from happening again. Susan, one of the guest singers, told Mary she earlier saw several boys coming and going through the door that could not be locked on the inside.

Dating Discussion Disrupted

The next program item was a discussion on dating. Tommy, a member of First Baptist but an infrequent attender, was quite loud, causing confusion with his questions and outbursts of laughter during the discussion. He had come to the lock-in bringing three visitors, Joyce, Mike, and Angela, with him. Not long after the discussion was over, Beverly came to Mary saying Tommy and some other boys were causing a commotion in the back of the auditorium. Mary promptly stopped the disturbance and warned Tommy that if his behavior caused any more difficulties, he would be going home.

Four Youth Disappear

Next, a film was shown which lasted about an hour. When the lights were turned on, Beverly discovered that Tommy, Joyce, Mike, and Angela were not in the lower auditorium. Tommy's cousin, Doug, was asked if he knew where the four could have gone. Doug said no, but he would go see if Tommy's car was still at the church. The four youth were found inside the car in the parking lot.

They all returned to the lower auditorium and were then taken to a separate room to discuss what was to be done about the situation. Mary asked for information about each one and discovered that Angela lived twenty miles away in a neighboring community while the other three lived in town. Tommy lived with his father, Joyce was staying with her grandmother, and Mike lived with his parents.

Three of the youth did not appear concerned about being taken home. All Tommy said was, "Call my Dad if you have to, but he won't be happy if you wake him up." Of the four, Angela was the only one pleading, "Please don't call my parents!"

Mary gave Jack a puzzled look and wondered how she should best handle the situation.

EXPLORING THE CASE

What are we going to do about the youth (teenagers) in the church? Who will work with them? For parents, pastors, and teachers, teenagers mean conflict. Where possible they avoid having to deal with them, particularly around issues in which they will encounter resistance from the youth. More often than not a special person is hired or a younger staff member is assigned to handle that area of the church's ministry. Parents are relieved. Everyone hopes no serious conflict occurs.

Lock-In is a case that explores some of the conflicts that arise around a ministry with youth, some of the sources of that conflict, and calls for some creative response. As you reflect on the case and how to manage conflict with youth you might ask:

1. What message does the church send to youth by delegating that ministry to a special person or a junior staff member?
2. How does the church handle the issues of authority and behavioral norms with youth? What does the behavior of the pastor of First Baptist Church—who carefully checks out the program for youth but does not become directly involved—say to the youth, the youth director, and the parents?
3. What is the most important issue facing Mary, the youth director? What alternatives does she have in dealing with the issue?
4. What conflict management principle would you suggest she try to practice?
5. What conflict management style might be most effective for Mary to use? What would it imply for how she should act?
6. Did you discover any of your assumptions about teenagers or adults and youth ministry? How do these contribute to conflict with youth or adults? What changes would you like to make in this area of yourself?
7. Contract for one area of action that, if carried out consistently, would change how you relate to teenagers or adults.

Possible Uses of the Case

- For an intergenerational dialogue among parents and teenagers.
- For church staff and lay leaders designing a youth ministry in order to explore their own attitudes and how these attitudes create conflict.
- For individuals, both youth and adults, to explore their own attitudes about each other, how they conflict, and different ways to interact with those of a different age and authority level.

CHAPTER 7

Ministry to the World

But he wanted to vindicate himself, so he said to Jesus, "And who is my neighbor?" Jesus replied, "A man was on his way from Jerusalem down to Jericho when he fell in with robbers, who stripped him, beat him, and went off leaving him half dead. It so happened that a priest was going down by the same road; but when he saw him, he went past on the other side. So too a Levite came to the place, and when he saw him went past on the other side. But a Samaritan who was making the journey came upon him, and when he saw him was moved to pity. He went up and bandaged his wounds, bathing them with oil and wine. Then he lifted him on to his own beast, brought him to an inn, and looked after him there. Next day he produced two silver pieces and gave them to the inn-keeper, and said, 'Look after him; and if you spend any more, I will repay you on my way back.' Which of these three do you think was neighbor to the man who fell into the hands of the robbers?" He answered, "The one who showed him kindness." Jesus said, "Go and do as he did."

LUKE 10:29–37

Operation Reach-Out (Growth)

ROBERT A. EVANS

Monday morning Dr. Fred Schultz hung up the phone, sighed, and meditated on whether it was not a mistake for Christian churches to set annual priorities for mission. As chairman of the governing board's personnel committee on the session of the Jefferson Street Presbyterian Church, this was

ROBERT A. EVANS is a theologian on the faculty of The Hartford Seminary Foundation, Hartford, Connecticut. Case copyright © 1973 by the Case Study Institute.

his third telephone call of the day from members of the church criticizing Sunday's service, which focused on this year's emphasis, evangelism. The views expressed ranged from "deep concern" to "outrage." The pastor's request the morning before that every member present "share his or her faith" by calling in the community immediately following the worship service was interpreted as "playing on feelings of guilt" or even "brutalizing the congregation."

The implementation of the mission priority of evangelism had disturbed and divided the congregation. Some church members supported the program as a vital and genuine response to the gospel and the community. Other parishioners interpreted this emphasis as a retreat from responsible involvement with social issues and thus a violation of the gospel. Concern was expressed over the adequacy of pastoral and session leadership. Members of both sides of the dispute were considering transferring to another church. Dr. Schultz, a professor of ethics at a city university, reflected on the reasons for this crisis.

Jefferson Street Presbyterian Church

Located in St. Louis, the Jefferson Street Church was formed in 1966 from the merger of Trinity Church, a congregation of 170 known for its community involvement, and Westminster Church, a more traditional congregation of 530 members. With the $90,000 from the sale of the Trinity Church building to the Urban Renewal Agency, the combined leadership of the two churches sought a basis for union. A statement of ministry was drawn up primarily by active members of Trinity but with some people participating from Westminster.

The original statement of ministry committed the church: to renew the style and content of worship; to develop an education program that deals with biblical, theological, historical, and contemporary issues; and to continue and nurture new ministries in and to the community. The present program of the Jefferson Street Church sought to implement their mission charter through a "learning community" involving diverse age groups and problems within and outside the church; experimental worship services known as the "celebration of the Good News"; and ministries to the community such as emergency food distribution of the common pantry, a tutoring program for ghetto children, a ministry to the gay community, and facilities and leadership for education and action groups on political, environmental, and housing concerns.

The Jefferson Street pastor, the Reverend James Wilson, later described the historical situation: "The general attitude was that this statement of ministry was not a very important document. Many felt that as soon as it was signed, the merger completed, the money and people in, life would go on as usual. However, there were people from both congregations who took the document seriously and it became the priority and focus for the new Jefferson Street Church."

Jim Wilson had been called one year after the merger from the position of minister to youth in a large suburban congregation to be minister of education and community at the Jefferson Street Church. Dr. Roberts, the senior pastor and former minister of the Westminster congregation, died six months later and Jim assumed all pastoral responsibilities. Consideration of calling a co-pastor with Jim was finally rejected for financial reasons and the church hired students from the local seminary to assist in pastoral duties. This year three seminarians were on the staff.

At the time of the merger, and following a re-evaluation of the active membership, the new church had approximately 430 members. By the end of 1972 there were only 200, the church having lost 50 members in the previous year alone. The congregation represented a wide range of age, occupational, ethnic, and economic components with a high level of church involvement across the spectrum. Considerable financial pressure existed due to rising costs and declining membership, along with the need to make substantial improvements to the building. However, total giving to the church was $9000 greater than in 1966. A struggle had developed at the last congregational meeting over a proposal to cut the percentage of benevolence giving. The mission budget was eventually restored when members of the church suggested and then agreed to take on some maintenance tasks themselves and to assume pastoral responsibilities during the pastor's vacation and study leave.

The Seeds of Operation Reach-Out

The practice of the church was to designate annual priorities for ministry and mission. In January 1972 the session established a new committee, the Committee on Evangelism and Outreach. Elder Donald Craft, being of Baptist and Quaker background, expressed an interest in evangelism and was made chairman of the committee. In a conversation with Jim Wilson, he shared his serious doubt as to whether it was possible to conduct an evangelistic campaign in a contemporary middle-class Presbyterian congregation.

The chairman planned to begin the work of the committee with a small group of interested members sharing, studying, and praying together with the hope that they would come up with some ideas that could be communicated to the whole church. Encouraging other members of the committee to do the same, Craft prepared a study paper on the theological rationale for evangelism based on the "necessity of witness" for the church as a "redemptive fellowship." He felt that an issue such as calling in the community demanded proper preparation with "more intensive devotional undergirding . . . more attention to strategy . . . and a commitment to meet together regularly."

As time passed the committee became concerned about an apparent lack of consensus within the session on the meaning of evangelism, despite the fact that it was a designated priority. Donald Craft declared, however, that "although the session, which evidently represented the mind of the congregation, was not ready to move actively in the area of evangelism, it could respect and to some degree support the program proposed by the committee."

On the other hand, the pastor was worried about negative comments he had received about evangelism and the general lack of enthusiasm for the program within the session. In recent years he had given special leadership to community involvement and service. At this point, wishing to express strong support for the new evangelism priority along with certain reservations of his own, Jim Wilson headlined the evangelism program in the church newsletter.

As the year progressed the committee did actively begin to do some calling, primarily on visitors to the church. However, general calling in the neighborhood was not pursued and so evangelism involved only the committee and a few other members.

Jim Wilson shared with a fellow pastor that he was perplexed about the unwillingness of the session and church to implement the evangelism program. Jim confided to his friend that the evangelism committee and the session were stymied over general calling. The session identified evangelism as a priority but when the program demanded the support and involvement of individual elders, they then began to balk. The phrase repeated in session was, "Evangelism is important but we don't have time to do it." Another reason, more significant in Jim Wilson's mind, was articulated by an elder in one of the monthly session meetings: "We are just not sure about evangelism. We don't like the word. It comes out of an old connotation; it was a bad experience." Another elder warned that the community would be very hostile to a general evangelistic campaign. The hesitation concerning evangelism that disturbed Jim Wilson most was voiced by an elder as a personal confession: "Perhaps many of us on the session don't know what we believe or whether we have anything to share. So we resist a program in which we may be asked to share our own faith with others." It was this attitude which seemed to deny a basic demand of the gospel that led Jim Wilson to take decisive action himself.

In December 1972 Jim presented a plan to the session to hire one of the part-time seminary assistants as an associate pastor in the area of evangelism. This pastor would have special responsibility for people in the five thousand new housing units being constructed in the area. The session subsequently took the proposal of hiring an associate minister to a called congregational meeting for advice. The session finally rejected the proposal on the basis that there were insufficient funds to add any new staff.

The Launching of Operation Reach-Out

In January 1973 the session reaffirmed evangelism as a priority, changed the name of the committee to Committee on Outreach, and appointed Joyce Nelson as co-chairman along with Donald Craft. A new and more ambitious program of evangelism, which came to be known as Operation Reach-Out, was also approved.

A conflict emerged now in the committee itself. Donald Craft complained to a neighbor that he had not been consulted on the proposal to hire an associate pastor for evangelism. He also was convinced that the pastor and staff had bypassed him by promoting a "dedicated young woman" who sought to usurp his role as chairman. Joyce Nelson's emphasis was foreign to Donald and in his opinion contrary to the basis on which the committee had been founded. Donald described the "new thrust" in evangelism as amounting to "a crash program to recruit new members." After attempting to share his concerns with the staff and feeling he had not been heard, Donald resigned from the committee.

Joyce Nelson, although relatively new to the life of the church, had been elected almost immediately to the session. Being previously associated with the Ecumenical Institute (an organization concerned with church renewal), she had been elected chairman of the session committee on worship the previous year and had moved into this new area of outreach at Jim Wilson's urging because of her "evangelistic" concern. Joyce revealed to a friend on the committee that she had tried to work with Donald, found it impossible, and so decided to get things done in the committee. Joyce expressed her belief that there was a need to constantly share the gospel with the neighborhood, and to involve every member of the congregation in this task. She did not understand Presbyterians who sometimes acted as though "they wanted to maintain the group they had and only invite a few others when it was convenient."

Operation Reach-Out, with the approval of session, was launched in January with a series of events: members of the congregation spoke in the Sunday service about calling on visitors to the church; sermons on evangelism were preached by Jim Wilson and one of the seminary assistants; and four Sunday afternoon seminars were held interpreting the meaning of evangelism. At the conclusion of this preparation period announcements were made in the church newsletter and at every service that there would be visitor calling every Wednesday night at 7:00 P.M. Also, it was indicated that on one Sunday each month, February through May, people would be invited to meet after worship for community calling and distributing of brochures about the church in public places and high-rise apartments.

Jim Wilson, in his January sermon in which he interpreted evangelism, had used as one of his texts Jesus' great commission from Matthew 28:16–20 "to make disciples of all nations." He acknowledged the negative image associated with evangelism in some of its forms. Jim declared that "evangelism is not a gimmick or a program, but a congregation sharing in its total lifestyle the Good News of the gospel. The sharing by Peter and John of the healing power of the gospel in Acts 3:1–10 illustrates what evangelism is about. It is a people who have found in Jesus Christ a new revelation of God, a new vision of life's possibilities, a new sense of their own worth, a new enthusiasm for worshipping and praising God, a new freedom. They, like Peter and John, must share the new realities that have shaken their lives."

So Operation Reach-Out began with statements and sermons. Twenty people attended the seminars, seven to eight people called each Wednesday night, yet on the first Reach-Out Sunday in February, only five people went calling after the service, two of whom were members of the committee. The committee and staff were terribly disappointed by the response of the congregation and so planned a special service for April that would incorporate evangelism into the service itself. The plan for a shorter service followed by calling was approved by the session and the details worked out jointly by the worship and outreach committees.

A Thousand and One Excuses

The sermon on March 18 was preached by one of the three seminary students on the staff, Ronald Smith, who stressed that "either one shared his faith or it died. As Christ is the bread of life so the news of the church of God's presence in life is the bread of life to the community in which we live." As usual at the conclusion of the service the congregation gathered around the communion table for the offering of life, gifts, and prayer. Jim Wilson broke the bread and the people shared it with one another. Jim said, "The call of faith is to share the bread of life, so we will distribute brochures that describe the church as we go out into the community. You probably have a thousand and one excuses for not going, but there are times when the faith demands that we act, and this is one of them."

There was a "violent reaction" to the service. Members declared, "We have been coerced" and "There were no options." Jim admitted he had "pushed people" to take their faith and commitment seriously, but he was "overwhelmed by the resistance and the guilty response" that were demonstrated. The service was attended by approximately 150 people and about twenty, including one visitor, went calling.

During the session meeting the next Wednesday, Jim and the seminarian were accused by an elder of "brutalizing the congregation." Another elder suggested that the service hooked people into calling by playing on their guilt, especially within the use of a phrase like "a thousand and one excuses."

Fred Schultz reflected on whether this was an inappropriate use of the worship service. "Is it wise to tie worship to evangelism or a recruiting activity? The church has nurtured a sense of freedom that allows one to say, 'No, that is not so important to me or compatible with my style.' " Several members of the congregation, Fred acknowledged, felt Operation Reach-Out might divert the church from more responsible and intensive involvement in community concerns such as educational revitalization and low-income housing. For Fred, a key issue remained unresolved: "In my judgment we have never been clear about what we mean by a 'priority.' Are priority issues exclusive? Must *all* members of the congregation be involved?"

Many members of the congregation, especially the young adult fellowship, had appreciated Sunday's services. As Joyce said in the session meeting, "Finally the demands of the gospel were clearly declared. Would any member of the session deny that sharing the faith is a necessity for a Christian? Besides, the general plan of the service was approved by the session and carried through by our own committees on worship and outreach. We must support Jim and Ron on this."

Donald Craft explained that he had withdrawn from the outreach committee in early February "in order to avoid a split in the church." In Sunday's service "evangelism was being exploited in the most crass way. This was no doubt done unintentionally, but it will reinforce people's earlier unfortunate association with sharing the Christian gospel."

Jim Wilson said very little during the meeting except to confirm the worship committee's approval of the service. However, because of their conversations that week, Dr. Schultz knew that Jim was discouraged over the lack of support and leadership provided by the session. Jim revealed, "I am more devastated by the move toward a 'no-priorities, no-goal' procedure for the church than I was by the personal attacks on myself. I may have made a mistake in pushing too hard," Jim confessed, "but there is a New Testament imperative to share one's faith. We have got to decide whether we are primarily a church or a social service agency."

An elder said, "We have confused 'sharing the Good News' with a 'membership drive.' The church has lost a balanced perspective that respects the freedom and commitment of each member. From this point on I don't want any priorities in this congregation—they only disturb and divide our community. Thus I move that we abandon the policy of setting annual mission priorities and that we announce our action to the congregation."

Fred Schultz had strong mission commitments of his own, and he respected Jim Wilson. He was convinced that good strategy required priorities, that faithfulness to the gospel did demand a response, and that the unity of the church was also very important. What was he to say? How was he to vote?

EXPLORING THE CASE

Conflict can occur as a result of differences on at least three levels. There can be differences in assumptions, differences in goals, and differences in behaviors to achieve these goals. Sometimes individuals agree on assumptions and goals, but disagree on the means to achieving these goals. Other times they advocate similar actions, only to discover that they mean something quite different by them, or hope to achieve radically different goals through these actions. *Operation Reach-Out* recounts the struggles of a congregation and the conflicts it experienced at all three levels. Since most individuals and churches have conflict over assumptions, goals, and behaviors, one can explore this case in order to learn different levels and sources of conflict, how they affect each other, and alternatives for dealing with these conflicts. You might ask:

1. What different assumptions about the nature of evangelism and how it should be carried out are present in the case? Which persons or groups hold these different views? What do these assumptions lead them to advocate as goals for the church and as specific actions to achieve these goals?
2. Which conflict issues are the most serious threat to the life and ministry of the Jefferson Street Church? How would you begin to manage that conflict?
3. What principles of conflict management would you like to see applied in the church, by whom, and in what setting?
4. Which conflict management styles are the principal actors in the case employing? Where do you see the issue to be primarily a matter of styles used, and where are the issues more a matter of assumptions and goals? How do styles and assumptions and goals get entangled with each other?
5. Are there resources of faith available to this congregation

and its leader on which they are not drawing? What
would you recommend?

6. How would you act in this case? What does it tell you
about how you manage conflict?

7. Identify some of your assumptions about evangelism and
outreach. Commit yourself to share these with others in
your church, and explore where you differ with them in
this area.

Possible Uses of the Case

• To explore the meaning of evangelism and outreach with
clergy and lay leaders.

• To educate congregations or their leaders on how to introduce change into a church, its difficulty, and alternative
strategies.

• For individuals to reflect on how they understand the demand of the gospel to share the faith, and the internal and
external conflict that may create.

No Room at the Inn (Mission)

RAY S. ANDERSON

Dr. Myron Amerson, pastor of First Presbyterian Church,
listened intently to trustee Mike Todd as he spoke. Todd had
just submitted his resignation over opposition to the outreach
ministry of the church after challenging the session to rethink
its proper mission in the community. While the other members
of session attempted to persuade Todd to reconsider, Dr. Amerson was turning over in his mind the factors that had brought
the church to this crisis and was considering how to respond to
this challenge.

RAY S. ANDERSON is Assistant Dean and Associate Professor of Theology at
Fuller Theological Seminary, Pasadena, California. Case copyright © 1976 by
the Case Study Institute.

The Background of the Church and Pastoral Staff

First Presbyterian Church, located on the edge of a large university campus in a West Coast city of approximately 111,000, was founded over one hundred years ago and reached a peak membership of 3,000 in 1961.

The congregation, preponderantly middle class, had a majority of members who considered themselves to be strongly conservative in the area of Christian doctrine. However, in a survey of the congregation, on a scale designed to measure openness to self-criticism and change, only 75 percent registered as "open to change." The style of ministry was distinguished by strong evangelical preaching, pastoral caring, and a reconciling ministry to those with divergent views.

In November 1962 Amerson was installed as senior minister. He had come from the presidency of a small midwestern college, and brought to the position a strong intellectual preaching ministry coupled with a deep social concern. In September 1964 when an opening developed on the ministerial staff, Dr. Kenneth Klein was added as associate minister of outreach. In addition to general pastoral duties, his job description called for his being staff resource person to the mission department with a specific focus on urban and ecumenical outreach. Klein remarked that he would spend more time outside the church than with church members. Some members eventually became critical of Klein and suggested that he overestimated the readiness of the church to support such a role on the part of one of its ministers. However, Steve Donaldson, who served as chairperson of the mission department, felt that Amerson himself had misread the congregation when he first arrived on the scene, expecting them to be more prepared than they were for engagement with social problems.

The South Campus Community Ministry

In the spring of 1967 an influx of young people from all over the country created an unusual situation for First Church. Because of its location near the university campus, which had become a center for free speech and radical life styles, over three thousand young people, primarily high-school age and many of them runaways, thronged the streets in the immediate vicinity of the church. Most of them, having dropped out of the middle-class structures of their own society, were expressing their disenchantment through highly visible and radical styles of life.

At a June meeting of the mission department, Klein announced that a study committee, tentatively identified as the Steering Committee of the South Campus, had been formed. It included representatives of the local neighborhood—merchants, citizens, street people, police, and local churches—as well as representatives from the United Presbyterian Board of National Missions and the Episcopal Diocese. The university was also involved on a consultation basis. He explained that the committee was an experimental effort centered in an old house owned by First Church, marked for demolition. Dave Pearson, an Episcopal seminarian, and his wife would be living in the house and would direct a street ministry designed to provide pastoral care and social guidance.

Steve Donaldson objected to Klein's announcement. He complained that the mission department had not been consulted prior to the announcement of the project and that this was simply another example of the church's staff moving too far ahead of the congregation itself.

Klein saw it differently: "We were simply under a mandate to create a task force to meet an immediate need, and we came to the mission department the moment we had something concrete to act upon."

Shortly thereafter, the steering committee identified itself as the South Campus Community Ministry and, backed by funding from ecumenical and national church sources, went immediately into action. Klein won a concession from the trustees to delay demolition of the house and the Pearsons moved in early July. The congregation quickly dubbed it the "Hippie House."

The response from the street people disappointed Klein: "The kids are leery of the clergy and the established church. Only a trickle come through the house. We need somehow to break the ice."

Accordingly, the directors of the South Campus Ministry,

led by Klein and Pearson, met the last week of July to plan a festival event to attract attention to the project. They chose a Saturday closest to August 14, the festival of the Virgin Mary, for its liturgical significance.

The Festival on the Parking Lot

The chairperson of the building and grounds committee gave tacit approval to use the church parking lot adjacent to the Hippie House for the event. A flatbed truck and a portable sound system were brought in. A rock band was engaged to perform, booths were built, Japanese lanterns were hung, and members of the congregation prepared food and brought used clothing to distribute free of charge.

The religious event planned for the festival took place at twilight. In addition to Klein, another Presbyterian and two Episcopal ministers participated, accompanied by two acolytes carrying basins of water and towels. They were garbed with vestments, ecclesiastical gowns with lace cuffs and colorful sashes. The group emerged from the Hippie House and made its way to the sound truck across the parking lot, which by this time was filled with about 600 people. Taking the microphone, Klein explained that they were there as representatives of Jesus Christ and the churches to be servants. Pearson read the parable of feeding the hungry and clothing the naked from the twenty-fifth chapter of St. Matthew. At that point, a large weather balloon with a symbol of the Holy Spirit printed on its side was released. Klein explained to the kids that they did not have to resort to drugs to experience the "high" of personal liberation. Then the four "priests" stepped down from the truck and, taking the basins of water and towels from the acolytes, began to wash the feet of the kids, kneeling on the asphalt. Klein felt that the event was the turning point of the street ministry, with hundreds of kids coming through the house in the weeks following.

However, on the Monday following the religious event the local newspaper severely criticized the sponsors and the churches for catering to the street people. The newspaper charged that illegal activities had been observed, including some traffic in drugs.

The Trustees Become Concerned

During the following weeks, trustees of First Church, Mike Todd, Roger Adams, and Ben Christensen, became concerned. After making some investigation they called for the closing of the Hippie House. Todd charged that the house had become a haven for runaway teenagers.

"Parents from across the country are calling, seeking to locate their youngsters, and the local police are coming by regularly, attempting to find out just who is staying at the house." He asserted that Pearson and his staff were refusing to cooperate with the police because they thought the police were unfairly harassing the kids.

Roger Adams agreed that First Church was being put in a very serious position. "I am a strong evangelical, but I believe that Christ has instructed us to render unto Caesar the things that are Caesar's." In addition, Adams expressed concern about First Church's possible liability to legal action. He claimed that the District Attorney was considering bringing charges against the trustees and families of the church who were harboring fugitive teenagers.

Klein pointed out that narcotics were being exchanged on the church parking lot whether or not the South Campus Ministry sponsored events there, nor did the ministry have any control over illicit sex. The staff denied that they were harboring known law breakers and insisted that their responsibility was to support and minister to the kids.

Pastor Amerson's Role

Amerson, meanwhile, had not become directly involved in the dispute. He maintained a position of neutrality and gave pastoral encouragement to his people and administrative support to his staff. He felt that his role was not one of taking sides but of assisting the process of creative conflict management at the level of responsible leadership. To one member he commented that the church seemed to handle missions better when they located in a foreign land, while the staff saw these kids as a mission at the doorstep. Amerson sensed he was con-

tinually walking a tightrope. On one occasion he was rebuked
by an elder for attending a student rally on campus that ended
in a disturbance. The elder expressed concern not only for the
pastor's physical safety but also for First Church's association
with such activities. Todd claimed that he attempted to take
Amerson over the the Hippie House to see what was going on.
"I wanted him to see the slogan they had painted on the wall—
'say nothing to the pigs'—but he refused to go in."

Amerson felt the controversy within First Church over the
South Campus Ministry was not a question of whether the
church had a responsibility for mission or not, but how to carry
out his mission. "A theology of mission is an essential part of a
'two-legged gospel,' " he said. "We have been standing on one
foot for so long that it is quite unsettling to some to have both
feet firmly on the ground. We seek to interpret events going on
around us from the perspective of the gospel and to carry out
an incarnational approach to our task. This often involves taking risks and taking our lumps."

On Friday afternoon, December 9, the trustees persuaded
Amerson to convene a special meeting at which these concerns
could be shared. At that meeting were several elders, the trustees, representatives from South Campus Ministry, the Chief of
Police, a representative from the District Attorney's office, an
FBI agent who was also a member of the church, and the other
staff ministers of First Church.

Klein felt that the staff was rebuffed at this meeting in its
attempt to present evidence of the positive results of the street
ministry under Pearson's leadership. The meeting ended with
an executive session including only Amerson and the trustees.
At this meeting the trustees attempted to convince the pastor
that First Church was headed in the wrong direction. "We
thought we had his tacit commitment to put an end to the project," claimed Todd, "or at least see that it was moved off our
church property."

The Resignations

As the session, the chief governing body of the congregation,
assembled for its regular meeting on the next Tuesday night,

Klein distributed a special handout detailing the positive results of the Hippie House ministry to date. Mike Todd protested, but the session received the report without comment. Trustee Roger Adams was not at the meeting due to a prior commitment.

On the agenda for the meeting was a motion supported by the mission department that the ministry of the Hippie House be given a three-month reprieve, with another three-month renewal after evaluation, and that the house itself be demolished after June 30, 1968.

During the debate that followed, Todd pressed hard for his case. "I don't feel that it is appropriate for our church to be involved. If one of you had a daughter who had run away, and you discovered that she had found refuge in a house owned by this church, sleeping on the floor with a bunch of other kids, wouldn't you have a complaint to make? We are trying to get ready to build a new church; it just seems impossible to have this kind of activity and division in our church at this time. I want to hold our great church together—it's a wonderful church—I don't see how this project adds to our ministry."

Another elder spoke up, "I agree, Ken Klein took several of us over to the house to see for ourselves the value of this ministry, but all I saw was a bunch of kids lying around in sleeping bags. Besides, the District Attorney, the FBI, and the Chief of Police all feel that we are cooperating with lawless activity and harboring fugitives from the law. Which side of the law are we on anyway?"

Klein retorted that law enforcement officials had not told the South Campus Ministry anything it did not already know, that there were illicit things going on all over, and that there would probably be some risks. It was up to the church whether it wanted to take those risks.

Bruce Bartell, a young attorney, responded, "I'm a relatively new elder and I am an advocate of the law, as you all know. But I wonder where Christ would stand in this? If we are hit, can we not turn the other cheek? And remember, ladies and gentlemen, it is the Advent season of our Lord. Is there no room at the inn?"

The silence following Bartell's statement was broken by a call for the question. The motion to continue the ministry was sustained.

At this point, Todd laid two letters on the table. "This is my resignation as trustee, and I have the resignation of Roger Adams as well to present upon his instructions. Unless the church is willing to dissociate itself from this kind of activity, which is being funded and controlled from outside the church, I cannot continue to support our programs. Our mission is to preach the gospel. This does not mean that we ignore social issues and human need. The church has a responsibility to challenge each one of us as individual Christians to implement the gospel through our actions. When we become too involved with clever new ideas we are in danger of losing sight of our primary purpose. I am sorry that our church has come to that point."

EXPLORING THE CASE

Much of Jesus' ministry was spent with the poor, the hungry, the social outcasts—those who were not in positions of social, political, or religious authority or influence. Conflict also surrounded his ministry. His action of reaching out, of affirming the dispossessed, of associating with those whom the religious establishment shunned brought him into conflict with the authorities and finally led him to the cross. The church compelled by Jesus' ministry has lived out the same conflicts within itself. On the one hand it seeks to nurture and care for those within its membership, and on the other to reach out to those in need outside itself. The issues around such conflict are rarely simple, but they are unavoidable.

No Room at the Inn recounts the experience of a congregation struggling to deal with these issues and serves as a paradigm of the dilemma of many churches. As you explore and learn from the issues in this case you might ask:

1. Is there one main issue in the case, or are there multiple issues? Are there certain issues no congregation can ignore and still be the church?
2. Who are the opposing parties in the different conflicts?

What common space are they trying to occupy that leads them into conflict?

3. What principles are evident in the ministry of Jesus that could be applied to the conflicts in this case? How would you apply them? Do these principles intensify the conflicts or help to resolve them?

4. In studying the ministry of Jesus, what styles of conflict management do you understand he used? Are these applicable in the case?

5. What conflicts does the case create for you? How do you deal with them in your own life and ministry?

6. Commit yourself to share these conflicts with at least one other person and explore how you might deal with them more creatively.

Possible Uses of the Case

- With a congregation or a leadership group to explore what they understand mission to be and how they might deal with the conflict certain decisions and commitments might generate.

- In an intergenerational discussion among adults and youth on an approach to caring and mission to help them discover what each group expects and wants from the other, where these conflict, and how the conflict can be handled.

- For individuals to reflect deeply and candidly on how they balance in their lives the call to reach out to the needy and how they get the nurture and care they need for themselves.

CHAPTER 8

Management of Ministry

So they came to Jerusalem, and he went into the temple and began driving out those who bought and sold in the temple. He upset the tables of the money-changers and the seats of the dealers in pigeons; and he would not allow anyone to use the temple court as a thoroughfare for carrying goods. Then he began to teach them, and said, "Does not Scripture say, 'My house shall be called a house of prayer for all the nations?' But you have made it a robbers' cave." The chief priests and the doctors of the law heard of this and sought some means of making away with him; for they were afraid of him, because the whole crowd was spellbound by his teaching. And when evening came he went out of the city.

MARK 11:15–19

Do We Need a New Pastor? (Leadership)

LOUIS WEEKS

"When he says jump, I'll ask 'how high?' " Tom Wilkins did not laugh when he spoke, but the tension lessened a little. Mary Frances and Rod Laughton smiled. Others sat back a little.

"Well, let's see if there is a way to get you to stay and work with Dr. Rogers," Mary Frances ventured. "The kids need you. The Sunday school needs you. We all do."

"I really don't see any alternative," Wilkins stated bluntly. "I don't want to leave this church, but I've just got to go elsewhere as soon as I can. Dr. Rogers beats me down, and I'll

LOUIS WEEKS is Professor of Historical Theology at Louisville Presbyterian Theological Seminary, Louisville, Kentucky. Case copyright © 1980 by the Case Study Institute.

need his recommendation—at least his neutral word—if I want to work in another church around here any more. So I'll just finish out my four months quietly and quit."

"That's why we're concerned, Tom. We don't want you to quit," Rod declared. The gathering nodded agreement.

Thomas Charles Wilkins had come straight to Community Church from seminary. He had been called to the Warrensburg church on the outskirts of Cincinnati, as the minister of education. The community of thirty-five thousand had begun transformation from its status as purely residential toward something of a commercial center in its own right. While the membership of Community Church had not grown over the past five years, it had remained rather constant at 850. Wilkins, Congregational in background, had appreciated subtle differences between the United Church of Christ and the Community Church. While the UCC was held together at a national and regional level by a cooperative denominational perspective, Community Church only belonged to a very loose association of voluntary churches in several cities. This individual identity meant that Dr. Rogers and the board ran the congregation's life entirely. Although the board, twenty-four men and women elected by the congregation, held monthly meetings, Dr. Rogers had effectively personalized leadership in the church for thirty-four years. As Fred Craddock, chairman of the board, said, "Dr. Rogers through his personal dedication, hard work, and drive to succeed made this church what it is." Dr. Rogers was also widely known as a preacher and author among community churches across the country.

As Dr. Rogers had overseen the growth of the church, he had personally supervised the hiring of a succession of ministerial assistants. Each had known that the "contract" would be for just a few years, and each of the previous four had been called ministers of education. Wilkins likewise had come as a "term" educational minister in 1975. He was to oversee the Sunday school, have occasional pulpit responsibility, and a portion of the calling on new prospects for membership who had children in the family.

Dr. Rogers's Heart Attack

Rogers, sixty-three at the time of Wilkins's arrival, had thirty months later, in November 1977, suffered a mild heart attack. Incapacitated for four weeks, and on a partial workload for seven months, Rogers himself encouraged Wilkins to take increasing responsibility in the church. Wilkins, just married and full of energy, had entered his new role with pleasure. No mention was made of the previous "understanding" that Wilkins would stay only three or four years at Community Church, nor was his position changed in title. (Neither minister had a formal job description, regular periodic evaluation, or stated performance standards.) The board did raise his salary to $22,000 for the 1977–1978 year. Wilkins had preached every other week. He had invited others on alternate weeks to lead worship—Dr. Miller from an Ohio seminary, and Dr. Thomas Reggins, a well-known counselor in the city. Wilkins had arranged the lenten services and special preaching by Willis Coleman, a minister of national stature.

During the time of Wilkins's service as *the* minister, he grew very close to a number of the members of the board. They spoke well of his preaching and his management skills. Fred Craddock, Chairman of the board, one night said as a meeting closed, "8:15! Why we've done our business and we're out in forty-five minutes! That's a record!" Several folk applauded as they rose to go home. Tom Wilkins had enjoyed the friendship of Craddock, of Mary Frances and Rod Laughton, of Bill and Mary Ward (who invited him often to their home) and many others in congregational leadership.

Dr. Rogers's Return

As Dr. Rogers returned to more active work in the fall of 1978, he assumed full preaching responsibilities again. Wilkins was asked to preach once a month. Rogers ran all the board meetings, though he seemed at times more rambling and vague than in previous years. Wilkins discovered some friction, as Dr. Rogers seemed to ask less and tell more about the educational life of the church. Wilkins began quietly to look for another church, but he found that similar positions in other churches did not pay $24,200 (for 1978–1979 he and Dr. Rogers received a 10 percent cost-of-living adjustment). He also realized that Dr. Rogers's health was not improving either. And Wilkins knew that not only could he lead this congregation—he already had led it, and very capably. In fact, he had several times commented to Rogers that God's providence was apparent, because in one person's problems another discovered strength and talents for accomplishment. Rogers had nodded and smiled when Wilkins said these things.

Change of Climate

Wilkins sensed something different in his relationship with Rogers, but he could not put his finger on the change. Never mind. With the busy life of the family, for Wilkins's wife Jan had begun teaching fourth grade, the year moved along all too quickly.

In May 1979 Dr. Rogers called Wilkins into his office. "My wife and I want to spend the summer in Maine," he confided. "We want you to take over again this summer. You know I won't be around here too many more years and . . ." Dr. Rogers let the sentence lapse.

"I'll be happy to fill in for the summer." Wilkins let the remark about retirement drop, not wanting to appear presumptuous. But that night he told Jan, his wife, that he now was sure Dr. Rogers meant for him to be his successor.

Again during the summer of 1979 Tom Wilkins preached frequently. He had called a meeting of the board in July when Ira Prentice's will was probated and the Community Church received $48,000. The law firm had wanted an immediate acknowledgment from the board of the receipt of funds. Two children of board members married in June, and Wilkins performed both weddings. Tom Wilkins felt capable, competent, and fulfilled. When Dr. Rogers returned in September, Wilkins submitted a rather full report, something he had not done before, and gave copies to all board members at the September 5 meeting.

Dr. Rogers referred to the report as "that paper" in derogatory fashion during the meeting, but he said no more that night.

On Thursday, September 6, however, Dr. Rogers called Wilkins into the office. "What's this about submitted reports!" he said.

Wilkins, astounded at the exclamation, for it could not be mistaken for a question, asked back dully, "What do you mean?"

"We both know what I mean. You are showing everybody here at Community Church that you can do it all by yourself!" Rogers's complexion was flush with agitation.

"Well, I'm just reporting on what I did this summer as you asked me to." Wilkins, too, became excited.

"Well, that's what Louis Evans told me. Exactly! Evans was in Booth Bay, and he used to be in Cleveland. He said to watch out for staff. They'll knife you whenever your back is turned."

Wilkins, defensively, said he never intended to undermine anybody.

"You'd better leave," Rogers said, and then picked up his coat and walked out of his own office.

Wilkins did not see Rogers on Friday, or on Saturday. On Sunday Rogers was to preach his "Welcome Home" sermon (as titled in the bulletin). But instead of the announced scripture (Rom. 8), he read the entire thirteenth chapter of Luke and said, among other things, that hypocrites in the church do one thing and say another, that Jesus felt forsaken, and that condemnation would today fall upon those who deserted the prophets.

Call for Resignation

Wilkins, on Monday, September 10, was again summoned to Dr. Rogers's office by Mrs. Ogletree, the pastor's secretary. "Dr. Rogers will be with you in a minute," she said, as Wilkins waited at the door.

"Tom," Dr. Rogers opened the door and greeted him. "I have come to a decision. You need to resign in four months or I will tell anybody who asks that you are a troublemaker." Tom

Wilkins knew that Mrs. Ogletree could hear every word.

"I will be happy to talk to you about the future," Wilkins offered.

"There's not much to talk about, and I don't want to get angry at you. You've been a good assistant, and I want you to have a happy ministry. I will help you if you cooperate."

Monday night, at the regular meeting of the Christian education committee, Tom Wilkins told Rod and Mary Francis and the rest about the outburst. "He thinks I'm trying to undermine him," Wilkins said.

"Why, if anybody quits, it should be him," Rod Laughton blurted. "He's sixty-eight and getting fuzzier all the time."

"Yes," Reinie Furguson, an older teacher chimed in. "We are convinced Dr. Rogers ought to leave and you should be pastor."

EXPLORING THE CASE

In examining cases or dealing with conflicts in real-life settings, remember that there are different types of conflicts: *intrapersonal* conflicts where the conflict is internal to an individual; *interpersonal* between two or more individuals; *intragroup* among members of a particular group; *intergroup* between two distinct groups; and *person-organization* when an individual has differences with a part or the whole of an organization. Since a key step in dealing with a conflict is identifying the primary issue, determining the type of conflict aids in clarifying the issues. And unless the primary issue is identified, one easily develops alternatives for the wrong issue or ignores key issues.

The case *Do We Need a New Pastor* is an excellent example of a setting that has several types of conflicts within it. One type generates another type and more than one type may be present in any one situation. You can use the case to practice identifying the different types of conflicts and how they impinge on each other. As you explore the case you might ask:

1. What types of conflicts are present? Make a list of the

conflicts. Identify the issue and the type of conflict for each.

2. What alternatives can you propose for each conflict? Can you propose alternatives that deal with two or more of the different types of conflicts simultaneously?

3. Who in the case is in the best position to intervene constructively and deal with a particular conflict? You might identify all the characters and decide what would be the most helpful action they could take in managing the conflicts.

4. What principles would be most important to apply in each conflict and by whom?

5. Are there resources of faith present in the case that could be drawn upon in dealing with the conflicts? What are they, and how could they be used?

6. Did you gain any insight into the types of conflicts you are experiencing in your own life? Have you, for example, been treating a conflict as if it was an interpersonal conflict when it was really an intrapersonal one?

7. Commit yourself to share one of your conflicts with at least one other person and explore how he or she might help you to deal with it.

Possible Uses of the Case

• With churches with multiple staff to train them in how they can work together effectively and how to manage their conflicts.

• With lay leaders and pastors to address issues of governance and how pastors are selected, evaluated, and retired.

• For individuals, both pastors and laity, to explore their own expectations of pastors and lay leaders, how their unexamined assumptions create destructive conflict, and how they might share these expectations and assumptions with each other.

When the Congregational Meeting Erupted (Planning)

CARL DUDLEY

"It's hard to tell the Christians from the lions," whispered the clerk to the pastor in the confusion of the congregational meeting. But Reverend Clayton Blake, the pastor, was too distracted to appreciate the insight. As moderator he had to decide what he should do next in a meeting that he felt was clearly out of control.

Background

Controversy was not new to Mid-City Church. Indeed, the stormy 1960s had provided the climate for the greatest numerical growth in the congregation's eighty years of Christian witness in that location. From the status of a struggling mission church in the 1950s, the congregation had utilized the challenge of its urban location to attract families and single adults from throughout the metropolitan area. Although the "Old Hundred" (as the earlier members referred to themselves) remained active and in positions of leadership, within only a few years the congregation had grown to more than 400 members, and a much larger constituency shared in the ministries of particular programs. In 1969, the Sunday worship attendance and per capita giving were more than double the denominational average.

Association of the church with controversial social causes had brought the name of the congregation into frequent public view in newspapers and other media. For example, when Mid-City Neighbors, a militant community organization, announced their lawsuit against the mayor and commissioner of housing, they did so from the front steps of the church. Such groups as Welfare Rights, Black Nationalists, and Resist used the church as a neutral ground for meetings of strategy with some groups and negotiation with others. In addition, the Mid-City Pre-

---

CARL DUDLEY is Professor of Church and Community at McCormick Theological Seminary, Chicago, Illinois. Case copyright © 1979 by the Case Study Institute.

school utilized the church five days a week, and the clinic was open three evenings each week, with special programs for drug abuse, pregnancy counseling, and legal aid for tenants. A food pantry was opened as a seasonal venture "on demand."

News media accounts of the activities and meetings of these groups did not always put the church in a favorable light. But church members often reassured each other and the pastor that such "misstatements and abuse only make us closer to each other."

The Change

In the early 1970s the congregation experienced a mild decline in membership growth, participation, and financial support. The inner life of the church continued: three choirs, full church school with four classes for adult education, plus the fellowship groups for youth, young adults, men, women, couples, elderly and for special interests. But Reverend Blake sensed a loss of momentum, especially in the causes and movements that had characterized the 1960s. He agreed with Warren Blackwell, an elder, who observed, "A congregation nourished on action cannot afford to drift too long."

With the support of the session (the board of elders), the pastor explored several approaches to encourage a revitalization of membership interest and commitment. At the same time the denomination, which was faced with a general decline in membership and income, sponsored a workshop, "Program Goals for the Local Church." Workshop leaders proposed a program of management by objectives (MBO) which they borrowed from the business community and applied to the needs of the church. The program suggested that members of the local congregation be invited to make recommendations for goals and objectives for their "life together." The session, with other members of the congregation, would sort out and organize these general suggestions into specific goals and objectives for the church. Then, in a special meeting, the congregation would have the opportunity to indicate which of the goals they considered to be priorities for the future of the church. "The church has been out of touch," explained the workshop leader. "This process gets everyone actively involved, until they 'buy and own' their decisions to support particular ministries."

Clayton Blake responded positively to the proposal. "It seems so similar to the causes and commitments that held the congregation during these past few years," he told Wayne Simpson, the clerk of the session. They agreed that this approach might provide "a handle by which the church could get a hold on its future."

The Session Meeting

In the February meeting of the session, the pastor offered the possibility of using MBO as a means to help revitalize the congregation. After outlining the basic process, Reverend Blake recounted the variety of ways in which goal-setting had proven especially productive for other churches, in evangelism, stewardship, and overall church planning.

Wayne Simpson immediately endorsed the plan. "In my business we cannot get along without planning," he said, "so I am delighted to see that the church is finally getting organized."

Several other elders reflected similar sentiments. Especially vocal in their support were chairpersons of committees in Christian education and finance. Warren Blackwell, chairperson of social action, spoke at length, "Too long we have simply reacted to emergencies created by others. Now, at last, we can plan our social action so that we can witness more effectively and really make a difference."

One reluctant comment was offered by Charlie Smith, an elder whose permanent seat had remained in the choir long after his tenor voice had faded. He admitted that he recognized some losses recently, but that he thought that the congregation was doing rather well. "Somehow I think that voting is out of place in the church, just for the sake of voting." He continued, "I guess that I hate to go looking for trouble."

Warren immediately reminded the session of the many decisions that it and the congregation had made during the past few years. He concluded, "It teaches adults to be responsible Christians, and children to share in our Christian democracy."

Charlie said that he did not mean to stand in the way of progress, "but this church is a family, not a classroom in political science." The pastor tried to summarize the discussion with assurances that a comprehensive planning process with clear goals and objectives had proven effective in arousing other congregations. He believed that it would do the same for the Mid-City Church. By consensus and unanimous vote, as with most previous session actions, the plan was approved.

Planning began immediately. Special committees were organized, which were not limited to the leadership of the session. The program anticipated: (a) suggestions from concerned people, (b) organization of material received, (c) voting on priorities, and (d) follow-through with new commitment.

In May it all came into focus for the congregation. Sermons, newsletter, and program inserts offered a variety of alternative programs and requested response. Other options were actively solicited from church and community groups. Leaders throughout the community responded with letters and comments. Publications were scanned for creative models from other congregations, which were clipped and displayed. More than half of the membership attended meetings in the homes of elders to offer their insights and suggestions to the church. Letters, scribbled memos, lengthy lists, and all other responses became decorations for the fellowship hall. Sunday coffee hour after worship became a seedbed of new suggestions, which were immediately discussed and often submitted in writing. Graffiti appeared on or near many of the posted suggestions. In all, the excitement and the color elicited the measurable participation of more than 80 percent of church membership and many non-members as well.

According to plan, the two hundred plus readable recommendations were distilled into thirty proposals in six areas of general concern. Many members worked with the elders in this process, and the results were posted for all to see "what had happened to their ideas." Then the proposals were translated into banners, posters, and dramatic appeals for presentation to the congregation. The presentations focused on choices of goals and objectives, not on specific, existing programs. The question was, "Where shall we go from here?"

The Meeting

The meeting, on a Sunday following worship in mid-June, exceeded the expectations of the pastor in every way—more people attended worship, more took part in the presentations, and more seemed interested in the results than Reverend Blake had anticipated. He had a sense of satisfaction during the presentations. To him, the content was appealing, the advocates were persuasive, and the choices were genuine and difficult. "Now," he announced, "we are all in a position to make concrete decisions concerning the meaning of the church in action."

Then the bubble burst.

Sarah Miles, past president of the guild, asked where she could vote for the women's association. The moderator called on the leader of one of the six areas that had offered the presentations. Joyce Jones, chairperson for area "C," responded that such a vote should be cast for item #17, "Study-Action Groups."

But Mrs. Miles persisted, "We are not a study group, but the oldest prayer fellowship in the church. And we raise money."

Another woman's voice assured the congregation, "We also study the Bible, which is more than can be said for some other groups which were listed."

The church treasurer chimed in, "There was no intention for the women not to continue to raise money just because they were included under 'study groups.'"

At this point two other women rose and spoke without recognition. "Why were the women *not* mentioned?" one wanted to know. "If we do not receive enough votes, do we cease to exist?"

The other women spoke rapidly, "We cannot be voted out. We exist! We have carried this church through more years than any other group." The moderator found himself fumbling for words of reassurance, for both the women's association in particular and the goal-setting process in general. Even as he spoke, it seemed to him that the list was suddenly much longer and more complicated than it had appeared before.

The treasurer, an old and trusted member, rose and spoke quietly, "Let us be reasonable. No one wants to do away with anything, especially not the women's association. But with limited resources we cannot do everything, all at once. We need your help in deciding."

Wayne Simpson added his hope that such a vote would make it simpler to organize the congregation, saying, "This vote will simply give us clarity and accountability in the work of this church . . . at last."

But the storm would not be stilled. Charlie Smith now repeated his view that they were a Christian family trying to make decisions as brother and sisters in Christ. He appealed for love and patience, and concluded with the promise of "a still more excellent way . . . " However, the resistance seemed to grow more vocal and widespread.

One recent member asked, "Why should we be voting on everybody else's business?" He went on to testify, "I know what it means to be a Christian; that's why I joined. But I do not believe that God stands for election, or that we can vote on his will."

Reverend Blake now noticed that several people were restless. A few were drifting out the side aisles toward the doors. But there were hands calling for recognition in every section of the sanctuary. As moderator he recognized Warren Blackwell, who had spoken so effectively in the past as the mover of social action recommendations.

"This church has lost the cutting edge of the gospel," said Warren. "We need to make those hard decisions within us that once characterized us in this community. God has called us, not just to love each other, but to make a difference in the world. I urge us to vote on these goals and objectives as our conscience directs us."

By the time his speech was finished about a third of the 200 members who had stayed for the meeting had found their way to the door. It seemed to Clayton Blake that half of those remaining members wanted to speak.

In this confusion the clerk leaned over and whispered, "It's hard to tell the Christians from the lions." Then he added, "What will you do now, Clay, preach, pray or punt?"

EXPLORING THE CASE

The church has benefited greatly from the work of the behavioral sciences. Organizational development particularly has contributed much in the area of assessment and planning, as well as conflict management. The use of organizational development techniques has also created controversy in many churches. Some have hailed it as providing important new tools for church renewal. Others see it as a secular intrusion that diverts the church from its theological and spiritual tasks.

When the Congregational Meeting Erupted is a case about an alive and mission-oriented congregation that wants to remain on the cutting edge. It employs some planning processes from the business world to generate new vitality. They appear to do everything thoroughly and correctly according to plan, but the process collapses into confusion, chaos, and conflict in the end. In using the case you might explore what differences there are between a behavioral science and a theological approach to church renewal. Are they alien to each other? Can they be compatible and support one another? You might ask:

1. Although planning attempts to be as rational and predictable a process as possible, are there extra or nonrational dimensions to the life of the church that conflict with the rational planning process? For example, what is the function of traditional symbols, words, liturgies, committees, names? How do these create conflicts? How should they be treated in a planning process?
2. How would you identify the key issues in this case? Which is most important and should be addressed first if the situation is not to deteriorate further?

3. What alternatives do you see for Reverend Clayton Blake? Who else might be in a position to assist in resolving the dilemma?

4. What conflict management principles would be most important for Clayton Blake to apply? How should he apply them?

5. What styles of management appear to have been used in the case? Did these contribute to the creation of conflict?

6. Are there resources of faith on which Reverend Blake and the congregation can draw to help resolve the conflict? What are they and how might they be used?

7. What did you learn about how you participate in planning in the church? Are your efforts constructive and helpful towards energizing the church, or do they contribute to the chaos? How would you like to change the way you function?

8. Commit yourself to one action that would make your participation in your church more constructive and faithful to the gospel.

Possible Uses of the Case

• With a congregation or a leadership group that is undertaking a long-range planning project.
• For a group of pastors or laity to learn about management in the church.
• For individuals to explore some of their internal resistance to change and the conflict it creates.

For the Love of Money (Budget)

G. DOUGLASS LEWIS

Pastor Robert Campbell stared at the letter from Philip Rizzo, a Dallas lawyer. Amalgamated Oil Company had gone into bankruptcy. Robert Campbell wondered what he could say to his church board, some members of the parish, his friends, and even to his wife. He remembered that only two years ago in the spring of 1978, the parish, on his recommendation, had hired Cal Richardson as its stewardship consultant. Richardson's personality and his program had captivated the Vine Street Church. He had increased their income from pledges and their mission giving, and he ran very popular seminars in family money management. But he also had convinced some members as well as Pastor Campbell to invest in Amalgamated Oil Company. Richardson had said, "The company has a fantastic future!" Robert Campbell, as he sat, letter in hand, reflected on his personal humiliation, his own values, the church's approach to stewardship, as well as judgment and responsibility in the situation.

Vine Street Church

Vine Street Church, located in a residential area of a medium-sized midwestern city, had in 1978 a membership of about 500 and an annual budget of $75,000. With a mixture of lawyers, doctors, bankers, and teachers, as well as white- and some blue-collar workers, it represented on a socio-economic scale a solid middle-class church. Robert Campbell had been pastor for seven years and was regarded by most members as a caring pastor and solid preacher. As the chairperson to the church council, Walter Miller said, "Campbell has the love and respect of our membership. They would follow most anywhere he leads."

A Concern for Stewardship

By the end of his fifth year at Vine Street, Campbell was convinced that the congregation should take its stewardship more seriously. He remarked to Tom Higgins, a friend, "We have the capacity to double our income, and increase our mission giving substantially. I am going to focus my ministry next in that area." As a first step, Campbell attended in the spring of 1978 a stewardship workshop led by Cal Richardson, a well-known stewardship consultant. He returned home full of new ideas and excitement. As a result, he convinced the church council to hire Richardson as a stewardship consultant for the

Vine Street Church. The council agreed to a one-year trial period.

Richardson's charm, knowledge, and approach captivated the council and congregation as it had Pastor Campbell. He ran a series of stewardship education programs, designed and managed their annual finance campaign, and trained them in a new financial reporting system to keep the congregation fully informed. During the finance campaign in the fall of 1978 the membership increased its pledges 20 percent from $70,000 to $84,000. Several special gifts to an inner-city mission project totaling $15,000 were also received. The council voted unanimously to hire Richardson for a second year.

Personal Investments

During 1979 Richardson offered a series of family money management seminars in the parish. They proved extremely popular among the parishioners. In addition, Richardson assisted a number of individuals in developing estate plans.

On one of his pastoral calls in the early fall of 1979 Campbell learned from the family that Richardson, during one of his estate planning sessions with them, suggested the family might like to invest some of their money in a company where it could really grow. Campbell felt some concern and immediately set up an appointment with Richardson the next day. The two spent three hours together.

Robert Campbell remembered well how Cal Richardson explained that he saw it as a part of his ministry to help people invest their money wisely and then to use part of their increased wealth for the mission of the church. Richardson shared that he had most of his personal money in a private foundation that was to be used to support the church's ministry. The foundation's assets were invested in Amalgamated Oil Company which, he said, had a very bright future. It was a company devoted entirely to the exploration for new oil. Richardson said he was a close personal friend of the founder and president of the company. Before the session finished, Campbell learned that Richardson had opened the opportunity to a number of the church members, some of whom were on the church council, to invest in Amalgamated Oil.

Pastor Campbell's Decisions

Robert Campbell thought all afternoon about his morning conversation with Richardson and then made two decisions. First, he contacted Walter Miller, chairperson of the church council, to suggest that the council should be informed of Richardson's activities. Miller was at first reluctant, since he was one of those who had already invested some personal money with Richardson. He agreed, however, when he heard that several other council members were also investors.

That evening Robert Campbell shared the day with his wife, Mary, and suggested that they too invest their savings in the company.

"It's a way for us to get that vacation home and provide for our kids' college, too," Robert urged.

Mary was reluctant but finally said, "I am basically against it but you have a better head for business. If you think it is best, I will go along."

Church Council Meeting

Cal Richardson came to the October 1979 church council meeting at the invitation of chairperson Walter Miller. Richardson shared openly concerning his foundation, what he knew about Amalgamated Oil Company, and why he encouraged people to manage their money wisely and how to invest. He reminded them of his stewardship philosophy, which he had taught in the parish for the past year, and the results it had brought. He even suggested that some parishes with which he worked had invested funds with him. He then excused himself from the meeting.

A long discussion among the council members ensued. Most were positively impressed with Richardson. Some even suggested investing some of the parish's funds with him. A few were skeptical. George Platt, who worked as a union representative, insisted that the council should investigate Richardson and his financial dealings. "We are responsible to protect the people of this parish," he said.

The meeting broke up late with no official action taken. Members remained long after the meeting talking about the events of the evening and speculating about their future.

Growing Anxiety

At the end of the fall 1979 finance campaign, Richardson's second year at Vine Street Church, the income from pledges had increased from $84,000 to $102,000. Richardson suggested they were on their way and did not need him anymore. He turned down an offer to remain for a third year, through 1980. Thereafter, Pastor Campbell heard little from Richardson. The tone of their phone conversations created unease in Campbell. Richardson became increasingly vague about the investments in Amalgamated Oil. Finally, in the late spring of 1980, he stopped returning Campbell's calls.

The pastor then decided to take matters into his own hands. Without consulting anyone he hired a lawyer in Dallas to look into the company. In June the letter arrived. Campbell's growing fears had become a reality. Amalgamated Oil had declared bankruptcy on May 1, 1980.

EXPLORING THE CASE

Money touches people's deepest emotions. It exalts and depresses; it creates external and internal conflict. The church throughout its history has also been ambivalent about money. Financial resources are essential to operate the church as an institution, but overconcern about worldly possessions strikes at the heart of the gospel. Many pastors have severe conflicts over money. Some are angry that they are not paid more. Others resent those who do have money. Still others conduct their ministries in such a manner, whether consciously or not, that they make people fell guilty about the money they have or the desire to have it. On the other hand, a person who appears at ease with money, who can make others feel at ease about it, or can

lift people's guilt or hopes about money, can have great power
and influence in the church.

The case *For the Love of Money* pictures a situation in
which a wide range of human emotions and conflicts about
stewardship and money are present. Encountering the case can
be an occasion to explore and learn from the conflicts money
creates for individuals and the church. In exploring the case
you might ask:

1. What are the various individuals and groups in the case
   seeking? Where do their wants lead them into conflict?
   What is the nature of this conflict?
2. From the perspective of the Christian faith, what would
   you say to each individual or group? Is the desire of each
   legitimate? Are there resources of faith to aid them in
   managing their conflicts?
3. What alternatives are there for Pastor Campbell? What is
   the most constructive thing he can do?
4. What conflict management principles would you use and
   where in the case?
5. What did you get in touch with about how you deal with
   money? What conflicts does it create in your life? How
   do you manage them? What would you like to do differently in this area of your life?
6. Commit yourself to an action that would enable you to
   deal with money in a manner more consistent with your
   religious faith.

Possible Uses of the Case

- For a stewardship committee in a congregation to explore
  the members' understanding of stewardship and their feelings about money and how the church should deal with it.
- For pastors to explore how they feel about stewardship and
  money, how they treat it in their ministries, and how they
  help others deal with stewardship and money.
- For individuals to explore how they feel about money, their
  stewardship, and their conflicts about money.

Index